P9-EGN-909

BETTER APART

ALSO BY ELENA BROWER

Practice You

Art of Attention

BETTER
APART

The Radically Positive
Way to Separate

GABRIELLE HARTLEY
WITH ELENA BROWER

HARPER WAVE
An Imprint of HarperCollinsPublishers

HarperCollins books may be purchased for educational, business, or sales promotional use. For information, please email the Special Markets Department at SPsales@harpercollins.com.

FIRST EDITION

Library of Congress Cataloging-in-Publication Data.

Names: Hartley, Gabrielle, author. | Brower, Elena.
Title: Better apart : the radically positive way to separate / Gabrielle Hartley, Elena Brower.
Description: New York : Harper Wave, 2019.
Identifiers: LCCN 2018029332 | ISBN 9780062689382 (hardback)
Subjects: LCSH: Divorce. | Self-actualization (Psychology). | Happiness. | BISAC: FAMILY & RELATIONSHIPS / Divorce & Separation. | SELF-HELP / Personal Growth / Happiness. | FAMILY & RELATIONSHIPS / Marriage.
Classification: LCC HQ814 .H327 2019 | DDC 306.89--dc23 LC record available at https://lccn.loc.gov/2018029332

19 20 21 22 23 LSC 10 9 8 7 6 5 4 3 2 1

This book is dedicated to everyone—dating, married, divorced, separated, divorcing, or separating—who believes their relationship could be just a little bit better.

Contents

Invitation and Welcome ix

Pause—Are You Sure You Need a Divorce? 1

CHAPTER 1 Designing Your Elegance: Dissolve the Myths,
Once and for All. 5

CHAPTER 2 Patience: Slowest Is Quickest 17

CHAPTER 3 Respect: The Stories We Tell Ourselves 45

CHAPTER 4 Clarity: So You Can Perceive
What Else Is Possible. 65

CHAPTER 5 Peace: Finding Calm Within the Chaos 87

CHAPTER 6 Forgiveness: Letting Go and Moving Forward. 113

CHAPTER 7 Need-to-Know Divorce Basics: The Elegant
Approach 137

CHAPTER 8 Don't Let Money Move You: Defining Your
Emotions, Desires, and Needs. 159

CHAPTER 9   Parenting Forward: The Legacy You Will Leave ... 185

CHAPTER 10 Really, We're Better Apart..................... 207

Acknowledgments....................................... 219

Resources... 223

Invitation and Welcome

———

You are cordially invited to revolutionize your perspective on separation and divorce. If your marriage or partnership is coming to an end, the book you hold in your hands is an innovative manual for cultivating presence and poise as you move forward. It's a map to your grace as well your growth for months and years to come. This is your invitation to quiet your mind, access your clearest thinking, and create progressive solutions.

Would you like this time to be the most intentional time of your life? Would you like to emerge from this moment centered in your most refined state of being? What if the end of this relationship were transformed into a powerful healing experience that prepared you to face challenge and taste sweet success? Dissolving your relationship responsibly requires courage, steadfastness, and emotional flexibility. As you'll experience, the content of this book will help you look back at this time with pride, having handled yourself with both agility and dignity. This is your invitation to practice five key states of being: patience, respect, clarity, peace, and forgiveness.

In my work in the context of divorce, I've observed clients and peers embracing a more positive state with quantifiable results. By dissipating negative emotions and consciously cultivating patience, respect, clarity, peace, and forgiveness, you'll more easily regulate your responses to legal proceedings, custody disputes, and other common triggers. By being more responsive rather than reactive, you might save months of time and thousands of dollars; you also might move more clearly forward on your path to fulfillment and freedom.

Since I began practicing family law nearly twenty-five years ago, helping families like yours transform positively within the context of divorce has been a privilege. Professionally, my goal is to help you craft a mutually beneficial arrangement for your family, boost your emotional health and that of your children, and counsel you through legal matters during this fragile time. I can say from personal experience that good divorce outcomes are possible, even in emotionally fraught contexts. My parents divorced creatively and consciously when I was a young child, and their choice to live around the corner from each other and visionary plan to share custody had a lasting impact that formed the foundation of the work I do today to revolutionize divorce as we know it.

As a longtime teacher of yoga and meditation, Elena Brower works to help you locate your grace, love the lessons, and ease your family's experience of this time. Elena and I are here to walk with you, offering guidance and our own professional and personal experiences. Having manifested her own graceful divorce, she offers you precise, potent practices in order to dissolve your fear, stabilize your heart, and design your family's calm future. Elena's path will be a beacon for your own, even at the hardest points.

In this book, expect to sense our support throughout your process. There will be bumps in the road, and it can get messy. Our commitment is to walk you through the five essential elements with easeful explanations and personal shares. You'll practice implementing patience, respect, clarity, peace, and forgiveness throughout your divorce process and into the future. You'll explore what you'll need to know legally, including selecting the optimal way to work with a lawyer and/or a mediator, and whether you actually need to go to court. We will delve into matters of your finances, parenting, and healing your mind and your heart. Handled well, your divorce will be a stepping-stone to your highest freedom and most conscious living.

Your Role in This Book

Shifting your state of being will take intention and effort. This process demands discernment, efficiency, and willingness. Right now, you might not have the time nor the emotional energy to read a long book with extensive instructions. So I've distilled my experience and advice together with Elena's simplest practices into clear, concise steps and prompts that will make a difference in your divorce and life right this moment.

You needn't be an experienced attorney, a meditator, or a yogi to be here; the tools in this book are designed to be accessible and highly efficacious for all of us. Our recommendations and writing exercises offer constructive, favorable shifts for you and your family.

Engaging in this approach takes tenacity and willingness, and the benefits are substantial. This approach is grounded and doable, with compelling examples and uplifting practices to help you move forward. Even if you find yourself in a state of confusion, anger, or sadness right now, you are on the precipice of a metamorphosis. When this process is complete, your elegance will light your family's path to higher love and courageous freedom. It's our honor to help guide you and walk with you.

BETTER APART

Pause—Are You Sure You Need a Divorce?

A s messy and complicated as relationships can be, leaving may not be the answer. A fresh mindset and some new habits can give you the internal power to meaningfully change your relationship for the better. While many of us may be better apart, some of us can actually become better together.

Separating may seem like a quick fix—an easy escape. Even if it is the right decision for you, please know that there is no simple solution. Before exiting, consider this: some of us can radically change our dynamic for the better from within the context of the relationship. An openness to small shifts in habits and perspective can make all the difference. Remember, while the shape of your relationship may change, your reliance on each other will continue if there are children.

Several times a year, I encounter clients who come to the realization that separating was not the answer for them. They decided staying together was the better option for their family. They realized that better did not mean perfect. Becoming better means recognizing where there may be edges to explore. Insights to gain. When our relationships become difficult, sometimes a step back is the best way forward. Staying and leaving elegantly both entail courage and fortitude. To be graceful and grounded with either choice requires that we go deeper.

We can transform our relationships when we are open to skill building. When we begin noticing what we can change and what we must accept. When we learn to take care of ourselves, listen to one another, and respond rather than react. Remember, as much as we'd love to change the people we love, we have only the power to change ourselves.

Consider the possibility that a pause, whether brief or prolonged, can offer unexpected benefits, even in the midst of a painful time. Where there was once deep love and commitment, there is also the potential to transcend even the deepest discord. The decision to separate is one that will impact the rest of your life, especially if you have children. It is a choice that deserves significant reflection and consideration. If abuse, such as untreated addiction, or mental illness are not in the picture, separation may not be necessary. The decision to divorce is not one that should be made in the heat of the moment. We're all imperfect: we communicate ineffectively, we misinterpret, we judge, we tell ourselves stories without really listening. To complicate matters, we're full of conflicting drives that seem to steer us in unexpected and unintended directions.

You might find that this book points you toward reconciliation. If there is even a hint that the two of you might be able to work things out, dare yourself and your partner to explore the practices of patience, respect, clarity, peace, and forgiveness as outlined here, prior to engaging with divorce proceedings. You may decide to commit to a period of time to work together to go deeper and explore how to make your relationship better together. Sometimes small tweaks in communication and effort to pay attention can make all the difference. This book might just offer the simplest solution to invite you to stick together rather than move apart.

Perhaps it's time to pay close attention to your partner, or to sit still for a week and just listen to yourself. Maybe it's time to check in with a trusted teacher, coach, or therapist and ask the new questions, design your life, and find out if your partner has similar wishes. Maybe you need to refine your active-listening skills. Maybe it's time to just look discerningly at your own role in obstructing your own dreams.

Consider the possibility that you can create a miraculous outcome via your thinking and your actions. Get a notebook or journal for our writing prompts and get to know yourself through your own words. If it feels appropriate for you in your relationship, as you go through this book, delve into each exercise and consider the space where there may be room for reconciliation.

Practice: Momentary Miracle

Take a seat on a chair or on the floor. Place your left hand on your heart space and your right hand on your abdomen, centered on your navel. Through your nose, breathe half of your breath into your right hand, then the second half of the breath into your left hand. Exhale fully.

Again, breathe into your belly first, then up into your heart, and then breathe out in the same way, exhaling from your belly, then from your heart, and finally out the nose. Continue to breathe fully like this until you feel calmer, more grounded, and steadier.

When you feel a sense of steadiness, imagine the most miraculous possible vision for your family. Is it a beautiful reconciliation? Or is it an elegantly wrought separation from which everyone emerges happier and freer? Write a short paragraph describing what a positive outcome looks like, and, most important, what it *feels* like, in the present tense.

Now note at least three actions, no matter how small, you can personally take toward making that vision real.

CHAPTER 1

Designing Your Elegance

Dissolve the Myths, Once and for All

You may now officially dissolve your misconceptions about divorce: the battle, the negative legacy, the stigma, the loneliness, the gossip. Starting now, *you'll* choose the tone of your approach. Regardless of what others are choosing, you can choose to be generous, gracious, and aware of the consequences of your actions. As a result, you may find that your post-separation dynamic is better than before, especially if you both engage in this process. But, even if you're the only one practicing patience, respect, clarity, peace, and forgiveness, your communications can become more thoughtful and functional—and you'll likely find that you're truly better apart.

No matter who initiated the separation or divorce process, your legacy depends on your inner attitude, your outer composure, and your vision for the future. While this is much easier said than done for some of us, there is simply never a need to speak disrespectfully to your ex or to anyone about your situation. It isn't productive for you or anyone else around you.

Having seen her parents endure a costly, contentious divorce, a woman I know vowed never to marry. She'd seen up close "how nasty marriage can be." This deep, lasting impression led her to "protect herself" by remaining unmarried. The real impact of this internal narrative? Unnecessary doubt, which led her to steer clear of deep relationships and live her life in a constant state of wondering what she's missing. When two parents choose to create a refined, respectful environment as they divorce, the children are more likely to retain a positive internal narrative about the possibilities of long-term relationships. Even if this is not possible in your circumstance, know that if at least one parent remains committed to healthy, supportive interactions, the situation can be markedly better.

While you may feel isolated, full of shame, or stigmatized, you're truly never alone in this process. Over the years I've observed countless clients in similar situations, on the same emotional roller coaster. And as you'll learn from Elena's recounting of her own initially challenging, eventually harmonious process, anything is possible. The power is in your hands, and the time is now.

After exploring the five elements of an elegant split, we'll examine the legal process and take a simple look at your choices. We'll explore the two biggest issues impacting most breakups: children and finances. We'll consider how to navigate the occasional post-divorce aftermath, even moving beyond your formal agreement.

Your Introduction

Patience, Respect, Clarity, Peace, and Forgiveness

No matter where you are in this moment, every aspect of your process is an opportunity to show up as your highest self. Even if you are deeply entrenched in a chaotic swirl of emotion, you can actually change the course of your life, starting right now. Through your choices, you have the capacity to shift the landscape for your family, your children, your body, your mind, and your heart.

The five essential steps to being better apart are simple, precise initiatives comprised of practices, writing exercises, and new attitudes. Even when you feel hopelessly stuck, with each step you'll find yourself experiencing the dignity of designing your stance and state of being. This will help you manifest the most refined outcome for your situation. As you read through these processes and goals, they may initially seem aspirational—perhaps almost impossible to achieve. Over time you'll find subtle, daily shifts from the inside out that will change the tone of your entire process.

Step One. Practicing Patience

The divorce process can be exhaustingly slow. When you practice patience, you infuse the process with calm, allowing you to take it one day, one moment at a time with dignity. Purposeful patience empowers you to listen, learn, explore solutions constructively, and let positive options in.

Patience opens up the path to true respect. Patience gives you strength to live in the present moment with mindful awareness. And when you practice patience, you're training your mind to transform catastrophe into an intentional future for yourself and your family. In chapter 2, you'll learn patience through practices such as mindfulness, personal reflection, and meditation.

Step Two. Practicing Respect

In every aspect of your experience, what you choose to see is what you'll receive. Should you opt to view this moment as a rejection or a failure, you'll continue to experience that repeatedly through-out your process. Should you choose to view this moment as an op-portunity to see through the lens of respect—both self-respect and respect for the others involved—respect will consistently reveal its gifts to you.

Respect for yourself, your humanity, your pain, and your process will help you begin to find respect for everyone involved. In chapter 3, you'll learn how to effectively take care of your physical and emotional health, so everyone around you is inspired to do the same.

Step Three. Practicing Clarity

Clarity is your capacity to receive and respond with lucidity, tak-ing nothing personally. On the journey from dramatic reactivity to nourishing responsiveness, clarity rules. When negotiating topics of gravity, such as your family's parenting plan, domiciles, and divi-sion of property, being clear about your priorities is vital.

In chapter 4, you'll learn how to separate wants from needs, so you can respond rather than react when matters get heated and feel overwhelming. You'll begin to notice which circumstances you can change and which may be relatively unalterable. You'll also learn practices to help you stand up for yourself and to assist you in get-ting what you need with compassion.

Step Four. Practicing Peace

Practices of peace present enriching alternatives to emotions like fear, aggression, and revenge. Peace implies a valuable neutrality that keeps you free of tension—in your body, your heart, and your mind. That freedom allows you to sustain your resources and keep yourself feeling nourished by your own attitudes and choices.

Practicing peace helps you reconstruct your separation or divorce as a sanctuary of new possibilities.

Step Five. Practicing Forgiveness

Forgiveness is a gift you give to yourself. It's a moment of giving up what might have been and realizing that everything is as it must be. Forgiveness in the face of even the worst aggression enhances your physiology, evoking a sensation of well-being and possibility. Forgiveness takes you away from contraction, toward an experience of expansion.

Forgiveness is a regular practice for most expansive thinkers; they know that holding grudges and casting blame keep people focused on fear, revenge, and destruction.

*　　*　　*

Each of these steps is here to help you create a pathway to being better apart. Patience leads to more respect. Respect helps you see your aim with clarity, which helps you cultivate peace. And when you're at peace with yourself and your situation, you're more capable of forgiveness. And where does forgiveness lead? To compassion, your ultimate innermost freedom.

From Practical Spiritual Wisdom to Legal Wisdom

Within each of the chapters on the five steps, we'll explore both practical spiritual wisdom and legal wisdom. You'll be introduced to each element through a mantra, or affirmation, to help you design your emotional state. Via specific writing practices in each chapter, you'll enhance your positivity precisely as if exercising to strengthen a muscle. To help you embody the spirit of each element, you'll also learn a simple yoga posture, along with a breathing practice or meditation. Then you'll also receive pertinent, relatable stories and anecdotes that will help you navigate the legal system and make sense of each step in your process.

Practical Spiritual Wisdom

Mantras, Breathing, Meditation, and Yoga

Let's take a closer look at the tools you'll experience throughout this book. Even if you are well versed in the practices of mantras, breathing, meditation, and yoga, reading these short passages is still a good idea, as each will help affirm your intention for mindful, positive growth during your divorce practice.

Mantra (Affirmation)

Take a snapshot of your mind in this moment, and you might notice a few statements passing through. Some are expected, but some might surprise you. Your thoughts are creating your reality; you're repeating something in your mind at all times; at any given moment, what you're repeating is your mantra or affirmation. The formal practice of using a chosen mantra in meditation involves the repetition of a potent word or phrase that yields the radiance and meaning of that concept until you experience a beneficial change in your state. We'll explore designing the words you repeat internally until you can successfully observe your own patterns of thought and then redesign what you allow to run through your mind.

For each of the five steps, you'll practice writing and repeating your mantra. You'll recite your mantra upon waking and before bed so that it resonates throughout your day and while you sleep. To keep these affirmations close, post them as reminders on your mirror, your computer, or your phone to be revisited as needed.

Breathing

In times of stress, anger, or anxiety, your muscles contract, your breathing becomes shallow, and your brain loses oxygen. With less oxygen, you're less creative, less adaptable, less responsive, and more likely to be fearful, aggressive, and unproductive. A few deep, diaphragmatic breaths will improve your mood and your mental performance.

Having counseled hundreds of clients to pause and take a deep, mindful breath during divorce proceedings, I have seen tangible results in my practice. One full breath is often the key to my client's ability to maintain composure and sustain forward momentum. Physiologically, one breath is all you need to access your most refined, solution-based thinking. Throughout the chapters, you'll practice accessible, practical breathing techniques that will help you stay creative and visionary.

Meditation

Practicing meditation has been scientifically proven to help regulate emotions, foster positive thinking, improve mood, enhance creativity, and increase feelings of happiness. Meditation is a primary daily practice, one that builds neural architecture that enables you to stay calm in the face of adversity. Such brain circuitry stimulates trust in your intuitive responses to challenging moments. As you accrue time in meditative states, your relationship with yourself will naturally help those close to you shift toward more grace and gratitude as well.

Yoga

In unifying your body's aim with your mind's resilience and your heart's wisdom, yoga practice improves your mental clarity, informs your perseverance, regenerates your wellness, boosts your energy, and increases your confidence. Yoga encourages you to listen and grow, to release what doesn't serve you, and to enrich the aspects of your life that nurture and nourish you. A mere few minutes of yoga each day, even just one simple posture, will help you feel present and ready to face the difficult moments from a more grounded, steady place.

Legal Wisdom, Not Advice

In each of the five steps, I offer legal wisdom to consider along with the laws in your own state. Why might you need legal wisdom in addition to legal advice? It's important to know that laws are different in every state; in fact, they can even vary from county to county. Hopefully you'll find the divorce laws in your state to be fair and favorable. Your legal process and outcome will always be improved by shifting your perspective. As I've seen time and again, your positive attitude toward necessary legal proceedings can make your split easier and more beneficial for you and your family.

Ideally, you'll engage in mediation or court just once. A lasting agreement is always, in the end, the fastest and least expensive option. Too often, however, couples repeatedly return to court because they didn't take the time to do their homework and create a thorough agreement the first time. Applying the practices of patience, respect, clarity, peace, and forgiveness will help ensure that you spend the least amount of time and money possible on lawyers, mediators, and courts—and that you emerge with a durable agreement that works for your entire family.

A quick look at two divorces will help elucidate the difference made by these five practices. The Waxmans and the Bennings are both divorcing in the same state. At first glance, their divorces have a lot in common. Infidelity. Custody disputes and wrangling over the splitting of assets. Toxic feelings. The soon-to-be ex-spouses of the Waxman family each retain a bulldog lawyer. They can't wait to get to court to show their respective loser ex who's the boss. Max Benning got himself an aggressive lawyer, too. But his wife, Lauren, retained a lawyer who saw things differently and asked her client to trust her and try a different way of divorcing that she termed *elegant.*

Both divorces are finalized. On the surface, the two divorces still look more similar than different; both marriages are over and everyone has moved into his or her new home. The splitting of the assets has happened in a comparable fashion, and the couples have each come to custody agreements. Look a little deeper, though, and the similarities between the divorces of the Waxman family and the Benning family disappear.

The Waxmans have spent thousands on court fees, for which each actively blames the other. Court was a painful, prolonged experience, creating even more feelings of fury, shame, and betrayal. Neither bulldog lawyer cared about any of that; this was business as usual for them. Because the Waxmans were unable to communicate calmly with each other, they never had a chance to collaboratively design a custody arrangement best suited to their family. It'll be a

miracle if the Waxman family manages to stay out of court, as both
parents remain consumed with anger, unable to talk about anything
else even as they attempt to build new lives. Their children still attend weekly therapy sessions and their behavior regularly merits
calls home from school. The Waxman divorce may technically be
over, but its shadow still touches every aspect of the family's daily
lives. Sadly, this is a typical scenario.

The Benning family avoided court and settled their divorce in
civil, productive mediation sessions. These sessions were powered
by the attitude of Lauren and her lawyer, who were deeply engaged
in an intentionally graceful process. Did Lauren's calm and consistent demeanor mean she had "forgotten" Max's devastating ongoing
affair with a girl from his dojo? No. But Lauren prioritized their
two young children, and her positive attitude earned Max's cooperation in redesigning their family dynamic. As Lauren discovered, the
more her husband, Max, felt heard and respected during the process,
the more open he became to looking at their split as a new landmark
in their relationship rather than as a battle with a winner and a loser.

The Bennings spent several thousands of dollars less on their divorce than the Waxmans did. Lauren left the final meeting feeling
energized, centered, and prepared for a future filled with joy and
personal connection. Best of all for their children, Max was now on
a similar path. The Bennings saved money, their sanity, and their
kids. By the time their divorce was sealed, Lauren and Max were
functional co-parents en route to a supportive friendship.

By shifting their attitudes and their relationship, Lauren and Max
made possible a supportive, growth-oriented environment for all
parties involved in the divorce. And this remained true for the du-
ration of their children's childhoods and even beyond. This is your
highest possibility as well.

Once you've learned the five essential elements, you'll explore how to find a good, forward-thinking attorney. And if you're already in the process, you'll learn how to work more intelligently and efficiently with the one you have. The different legal approaches to a divorce will be discussed, as well as why you'll want to consider avoiding court and how you can make that happen. And if you must go to court, I'll set you up for the best possible outcome, with practical tips to help you keep calm, centered, and creative.

You'll also learn how to address your assets and debts, and how to create a sustainable parenting agreement that nurtures your entire family. You'll learn how to create a viable blended family while navigating holidays, birthday parties, dating, and friendships with ease. In the long run, taking the time to acknowledge and manage your split with as much care as you took when you came together will benefit everyone involved. Your ingenuity and willingness to craft an agreement that suits your whole family will reverberate into the future as trust, tranquility, and true freedom.

CHAPTER 2

Patience

————

Slowest Is Quickest

The hour of fulfillment is buried in years of patience.
—MARY OLIVER

There is a very good reason for starting with patience. You simply can't get divorced without enduring some lengthy process of some kind, be it emotional, physical (division of actual property), or legal. Partly by design, and partly because courts are incredibly backlogged, the wheels of justice move notoriously slowly. Despite the myths, there's really no such thing as a quickie divorce. And even if the legal process ends up being super-efficient and fast for you, dealing with the emotional aftermath may still take considerable time.

Through years of working in the legal system with families undergoing divorce, I have found that patience is the most crucial tool for endurance. Patience will usher you through your process with ease and respect. Patience is your ability to wait—sometimes way longer than you'd hoped—with trust and steadiness. Especially in times of great stress, patience is as nourishing for your mind as it is for your body. The practice of patience is an exercise in learning to sit with what is challenging and allow time for things to settle and realign.

The quiet power of patience is there to help you shift your attitude and redesign your relationship to your ex-partner, your family, your community, and yourself. You'll be glad to draw upon your cultivated reserves of patience as you wait to hear from the lawyers, the mediator, or your ex. You will need patience waiting for your next court appearance or meeting. When a law seems confusing or grossly unfair, your practice of patience will guide you to an acceptance of the law even in light of its apparent or inherent unfairness. And, of course, patience has innumerable applications in matters of the heart.

With the practice of patience comes the capacity to respond with productive intention rather than to react impulsively to situations that trigger negativity. In the context of divorce, measured responsiveness to emotions like anger or sadness is highly stabilizing. Recall a situation highly charged with emotion in which you reacted impetuously, which only made things worse. With patience, a difficult emotional experience can be a powerful catalyst for positive personal growth. Rather than some intuitive gift with which you were born, patience is a muscle you're developing. Strengthen your patience and you'll see its effects on other areas of your life as well.

In the early days of Elena's divorce, she only wanted to rush it, to hasten the process in order to ease her pain. Before she realized that elegance was an aim for her process, she was not patient and nearly destroyed the future friendship she's now built with her son's dad. Here's what she told me when we first began working on this book.

I had to practice consciously changing my attitude and continuously try on the perspective of patience. It wasn't natural for me; I wanted to get the divorce done and move on. I actually wanted to stay in pain and stay angry. I caused fights, choosing my addiction over my healing for months. I remember specific situations when I was weak, troubled, and difficult with my son's dad and others. I was defensive, destructive, and afraid.

I started practicing more yoga, more meditation, and I sought coaching so I could learn how to offer myself and my family a steady, reassuring space. When I started being patient with myself, I found that I could be far more attentive to my son's dad, which helped him feel heard, and we all began to land in a more mindful place. There were still many moments when I could hear my mind's default words of frustration and fear bubbling to the surface, but the patience practices I was learning helped me turn to myself, rewrite my inner commentary in the moment, and trust the process so I could be outwardly softer. Then in time my interior space softened, too.

If my experience is any indication, consciously developing a steady internal patience for your own process means you're more likely to arrive at an environment (and ultimately an agreement) that makes lasting sense for your family. By learning how to be present and patient with the most extreme emotional discomfort, which might take weeks or even months, you'll learn one of the most valuable aspects of true elegance: responding calmly rather than overreacting. By resisting reactive, impulsive attitudes, you're far more able to arrive at a sensible big-picture solution that works best for your family, at any moment.

Developing a Practice of Patience

Patience Begins with You

Developing a practice of patience must always begin with you. Chaos is all around you, and likely part of your daily inner dialogue. Karin, a stay-at-home mom of two in her late thirties, was unclear where to begin. Her world was falling apart. Her husband revealed he was no longer interested in working on their marriage, and she wanted to understand what went wrong. She was scared that her husband would insist on staying in the marital house, which meant that she'd have to move—but she had no money to get another home.

The custody arrangement had not been discussed, and she was afraid he might try to take the kids. She was a nurse, but she hadn't worked for years. She was sure that it would be impossible to get relicensed, and she was deeply concerned about her finances. Karin thought that she would never be able to support herself without his help. Based on a friend's experience, she feared that the kids could be turned against her because her husband had more spending power and could treat them to more of what they wanted. Maybe they would even tell the therapist that she was a bad mother. What if the kids needed a lawyer, too? How could she support herself through all of this? Plus, her mother had fallen ill. It was all just too much. I helped her slow down her own mind so she could begin to engage meaningfully and go beyond the cycle of doubt, fear, and haste.

I offered Karin the idea of addressing one small aspect at a time. One issue each day, or each week, as long as needed; eventually the entire picture would become clear. She agreed. I mapped out with her a simple chart for each item to break down the swirl and remove the anxiety. Next we talked about which element was causing her the most stress and which was the most easily addressed. We decided it made the best sense for her to chip away at the easier parts first. In time everything came together.

She reached out to her siblings, who began to take over for her extra shifts with her mother. I called her husband's lawyer and made an arrangement for him to pay for Karin's initial legal fees. We had a sit-down meeting with her husband and his lawyer, and arrived at a preliminary plan for co-parenting. Her husband agreed not only to pay child support but also to help her pay for her recertification as a nurse. Bit by bit the chaos abated and her life started to come together. After she had settled down, she realized she didn't actually want the house. She wanted to move downtown and simplify her life. Karin felt lighter than she had in years.

The Patience Circles

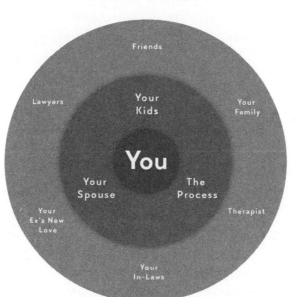

By prioritizing patience and taking things one at a time, she was able to curb her anxiety and move through this difficult time bit by bit until her whole life was reconstructed, even better than before.

For when you are practicing patience, Elena and I have devised a simple map of concentric circles that emanate out from the center. Each one of these circles has within it a handful of influences in your life. She recommends first seeing yourself at the center of the map. Then just beyond you are your children, your ex, and the process. And then, on the next circle are your family, friends, lawyers, and so on. As you move forward, you'll adjust your relationships so that they beneficently fit into your life positively. You'll allow new relationships to enter, and you'll likely let some of the others go. What's helpful is to simply recognize the constant at the center of that map: YOU.

> You are the one unchanging factor. Once you realize that you are also the only aspect of this map over which you have any control, you'll begin to compose yourself, so that what you want will more likely come to you. Practice: First, acknowledge to yourself that this is your moment to move toward to invite patience into your mind, heart, body, and soul. The door is open. Notice how you feel. The sweetness that arises when you take a little extra time to be present and patient for yourself will serve as a balm to your entire family.
>
> Develop patience with yourself, for your feelings and your actions, by taking things slowly, moment to moment, day to day. This simple practice will teach you how to be patient with everyone else in your life. An easy and effective way to invite more patience into your life is to move more slowly in your daily tasks, like cleaning, working, washing dishes, and eating.

Mantras for Patience

Next, try seeding your patience practice with words and phrases imbued with exactly the right energy for supporting your intention to be patient. Elena has created a set of mantras or affirmations for patience that you may use at any time. It's a good idea to use the mantras several times daily, to affirm the new states of being you're welcoming into your life. Begin and end your day with a mantra for patience and repeat one internally or aloud whenever you feel impatience lurking at the edges of your thoughts.

Practice these affirmations in the silence of your own mind, note them in your journal, even say them aloud. If you feel comfortable sharing these with your ex, attorney, or mediator, maybe they too will find this interesting. Let these affirmations or mantras usher in the sensation of patience to your mind and body. Choose one or two that resonate and keep those close.

In order for this practice to become truly transformative, it must be established as a part of who you are, your daily routine, integrated into your ways of thinking and being. If you feed yourself negative messages, the likelihood is that you'll feel pretty bad. When you feed yourself positive, affirming thoughts, ideas, and opinions, you're nourishing the part of your brain that keeps you calm, contented, and clear. Once you're in the habit of engaging yourself in a more positive inner dialogue, your daily thoughts will begin to transform effortlessly. With a steady, regular practice, you will find that your daily affirmation will become part of who you are, integrated into your world view.

Commit to selecting one mantra for patience and recite it at least several times a day. Repeat it silently to yourself in the morning when you arise, at any point during the day when you notice you're feeling anxious or triggered, and at night before bed. Take a deep breath in, and when you reach the fullest part of the inhalation, hear your mantra as you slowly exhale. Repeat this three times before moving back to your regular activity.

> *I am responsive, collected, and calm.*
> *The present moment is the only moment I can control.*
> *I patiently allow this negative thought to pass me by.*
> *I carefully consider all possibilities.*
> *Patience is my choice, my aim, and my journey.*
> *I prioritize happiness in my family.*

Mantras set the stage in your body and mind for the radical change you wish to invite into your life. Get comfortable using patience mantras, and know the ones that resonate most meaningfully with your heart.

Transmitting Patience:
It Begins with You

Patience for yourself, for your kids, for your ex, and for the ongoing legal process is now finding a place in your heart. And once it has been established, your entire environment will become more easeful and manageable. This can happen faster than you might expect, and it's critical to your happiness and healing. Take a look at the circles again. Notice who or what is in closest proximity to you within the circles. Notice where you can be more patient with those people or in those arenas. Work on developing your patience bit by bit as you move out from the center.

Reread this section when it feels like the cards are stacked against you, whether at work, at home, with your legal case, or with your-self. Reread this when you just want this whole experience to be over *now*. Reread this when you feel like you have way too much to manage and there is no way you can possibly tackle it all or even see past this stage of your life. As soon as you've read this, even multiple times, you'll be reminded to incorporate patience into your conscience. And when a day at a time is too much, try tackling patience hour by hour. If that's still too much, just try moment by moment.

PATIENCE WITH YOUR KIDS. In many instances, a child may take sides. Both Elena and I have witnessed a child shunning one parent for the other during the divorce process. If the parent who's being shunned stays tender, patient, and present, in time the child will recognize that steadiness and come back. Children are much more resilient and capable of seeing the truth than we imagine. You'll find more on this in chapter 9, which is devoted to nurturing your family. Elena has a technique to locate patience during the toughest moments.

Close your eyes for a moment and imagine being your child's age. Really take a moment to imagine yourself in your child's shoes. How is your divorce impacting her or him? In the best-case scenario, your children love and depend on you both, or at least you, so bear in mind that a feeling of being inwardly highly conflicted will likely cause your children to act out of character from time to time. Do this for each of your children, and you may even wish to take notes. Their lives matter here, too, and if you can set the example for patience by being patient with them, you'll be setting them up for success for life.

PATIENCE WITH YOUR EX-PARTNER. No matter how the divorce is turning out, set the example of thoughtfulness for your kids and their future relationships by being patient with your ex. The fuel that you add to the fire won't help; as time passes, the heat of this moment will dissipate. Practice letting it cool down. If you're on the receiving end of the divorce, unpalatable as it may sound, it could be helpful to recognize that this is likely uncomfortable for your ex, too. You both need to let this new reality sink in. Give yourself the gift of time.

Elena suggests that you compose and write down a list of what you wish you could do when you're feeling particularly provoked. For example, "I wish I could make this all end. I wish I could be sitting in my new house with my new life in my new town. I wish I could stop thinking about this." Keep writing until you've put down everything you can think of. Then set a timer for at least thirty minutes before doing anything at all in regard to your ex—no texting, calling, nothing. By that time, the heat will have begun to dissipate, and the moment will be passing.

PATIENCE WITH THE LEGAL SYSTEM. I can't tell you how many people come in complaining about the law, their kid's therapist, the ex's lawyer, the judge. As you move through this process, accept the system and its players, imperfect as they are. Recognize that all the players (including the law) are functioning in the best possible way, here and now. When there is little or nothing you can do to shift the law or the players—unfair or otherwise disagreeable as they may feel—do your best to be patiently at peace within yourself.

Practices such as movement, writing, breathing, and meditation will help you orient yourself within this new reality. Below the specific practices, you'll find some typical examples of how and when you might find these tools useful. Feel free to be creative and come up with your own.

Movement and Postures for Patience

Experts on resilience believe we all have the power within ourselves to manage any circumstance. Renowned social psychologist Dr. Amy Cuddy argues that we can significantly change the way our future unfolds by repeatedly doing this simple two-minute power pose. Raise your chin and throw your arms straight up in the air, just as athletes do when they experience victory. Breathe there until you feel uplifted. This power pose, first presented during Dr. Cuddy's celebrated TED Talk, which has since garnered more than forty million views, enables our minds to change our bodies, and our bodies to change our minds for the better.

Cuddy demonstrated that by tweaking body language, we can change our outcome. We can create success in whatever challenge stands before us. When they exhibited the power pose for just two minutes, they were more likely to succeed in whatever task or challenge stood before them. When they sat slump-shouldered, heads down, displaying uncertainty, the opposite happened. Bottom line: reach high, stand tall, and you will positively shift the world within and around you.

"Tiny tweaks," says Cuddy, "can lead to big changes." I often send clients to the restroom during stressful divorce negotiations to try this pose, asking them to hold the position for several long, deep breaths, especially if it feels awkward. And it always helps them shift away from negativity and into a more positive mental space.

Elena has two simple postures for when things feel emotionally or logistically unfair at this moment and seem to be out of your control.

Find a wall nearby and close the door. Lie down on your back with your bottom close to the wall; then extend your legs straight up the wall. Allow your feet to gently fall open to the sides. Place one hand on your belly and one hand on your heart space. Let it all go upside down and quiet your thinking mind for a few minutes. If it feels right, use your mantra here as you exhale and let it sink in. Treating yourself to a moment of seeing things differently, without judgment or fear, will actually help you function patiently amid the chaos of your mind and your current world.

Elena offers this posture for your desk chair or anywhere you are seated, as a way to calm your system and make room in your body when you feel anxious or constricted.

First, inhale to lift your right shoulder toward your right ear and hold it for a moment; exhale as you let the shoulder drop. Then inhale your left shoulder to your left ear and hold that breath in momentarily; exhale to let the shoulder release. Inhale both shoulders as high as you can and hold that breath in for an extra moment or two, as long as it's comfortable—and then exhale. Inhale and hold for a moment, then exhale. Feel that shift and slowing. Release both shoulders to relax. Repeat as often as you wish.

Then interlace your fingers behind you and roll your upper arms together as you inhale a long, deep breath, lengthening your spine as you hold that breath and smile for a moment. Then exhale as you relax your entire body, releasing your arms at your sides. Once more: interlace, inhale, lengthen, and smile—then exhale, release, and relax. Let your hands rest on your thighs and take a couple more natural breaths to observe if things have softened a bit.

Writing Your Patience

Sit in a comfortable, quiet place with your journal. Rather than feeding the negative loop that you may have running in your mind, reflect for a moment on the ideal outcome for your divorce and then write it down. And strangely enough, I'm going to ask you to write this ideal outcome in the present tense, as though it's already happening and complete. Be descriptive, thorough, and ready to surprise yourself; you're setting the stage for the ideal outcome. You'll save that description as you shift your intent throughout your process.

As Elena shares some of her story, try to envision your own patience with each phase of your process, from this moment to the finish line for your family. Elena suggests you consider the following questions once you've read her story. After you've read her words below, set a timer for ten minutes and write your story with these questions in mind:

How would you tell your story in the most optimal and constructive way?

If you could lose your sadness, anger, fear, and dread, what would be left?

Where are the important lessons, sacred learnings, or difficult truths you're exposing in this shift in your life?

THE FIRST NIGHT. Realizing that my life is crumbling. Calling my women friends to share the "shameful" news. Seeking numbness in my addiction. Sleepless nights, reactive behavior, vain attempts at faked kindness, my own sheer blindness to the part I'd played in this outcome.

THE FIRST WEEK. Coming to understand that fragility is medicine, too. Vulnerability is helpful. Nothing is what it seems. Aiming all my arrows at patience and forgiveness.

THE FIRST MONTH. Learning to be compassionate with myself as a practice. Understanding that my own actions had fed this current reality; knowing that I can be forgiven, and so can he. Feeling the truth of being set free, beginning to sense that we'd all land happily in this new life, as teachers of compassion rather than mediocrity. We'd be leaders of great communication and solidarity, as a family. This is when I begin to see my own patience clearly.

THE FIRST YEAR. Telling my then four-year-old son the same story, night after night—the story of a girl called Elena, who'd met her dream man sitting in her yoga class, whom she'd marry within months. A handsome, beautiful being with whom she knew she must have her baby boy, Jonah. A soulful man whom she'd realize within a few short years that she was meant to be friends with rather than married to. A best friend whom she'd come to understand would be family until the end of time.

*   *   *

It's been more than eight years since then at the time of this writing. What initially felt like the worst nightmare of my adult life has become a growing partnership and deepening friendship. Jonah's dad feels like a brother to me. Sometimes when I consider where it's been and where it's going, I could cry with gratitude, knowing that our attitudes have generated this miraculous reality. I couldn't have imagined that my divorce, managed with dignity, would end up revealing the very best of me.

Now go back to the questions on page 29. Craft your responses in the present tense.

Breathing for Patience

Breathing is the most basic and essential and effective way to reduce tension and calm yourself. I routinely offer this practice to my clients to help them stay present during more difficult meetings. This often prevents them from overreacting to outrageous statements from any of the participants or from making disrespectful or quizzical faces when in front of the judge. A few simple deep breaths may be just the medicine you need to prevent yourself from wanting to toss a cup of water across the table at a difficult meeting.

Here are Elena's thoughts on breathing for patience:

Wherever you are, take a few quiet moments to breathe consciously as you read these words. No forcing your breath; simply relax your mind enough to follow the movement of your breath from your nostrils into your belly. As you breathe in and out through your nose, notice your breath skimming along your soft palate (the roof of your mouth), softly descending into your belly. The breath is a perfect reflection of your mind. As your breath becomes more quiet, your mind becomes more balanced. As you relax further, your breathing will become softer and more shallow. Spine tall, continue to watch your breath. Notice your breath becoming increasingly quiet, increasingly subtle. By the fourth or fifth breath, you'll be less likely to be reactive and more likely to consider, choose, and create.

Meditation for Patience

Slowest Is Quickest

During the course of her divorce, Elena received an important lesson from a healer who has made a strong and lasting impression on her life. "Slowest is quickest, Elena." While she didn't grasp it at first—and, in fact, felt an aversion to the truth of it—she's beginning to embody it now, almost a decade later.

She notes, "When I move with precision and grace, what needs to happen can happen more readily. My haste, with regard to professional projects or in the most daily moments, was running the show and ruining my inner state. Via deliberate movement and daily breathing practices, I now can change a feeling of urgency into a feeling of connection and communication. No matter where you are, when you feel impatient, I have one quick practice you may do in plain sight to help turn you around and give your mind some space from the haste you're feeling."

Practice

If you're sitting or standing, simply place your hands flat against your heart. This happens to be one of my favorite mudras, or hand placements, with left hand flat to the center of the chest, then right hand on top of that.

It places your attention back inside and helps you remember yourself, your connection to what's important, to what heals. Once your hands are there, take a huge inhale right into them, and when you exhale, as the air releases out of your nostrils, gently invite your navel back toward your spine. Take two more full breaths just like that—into your hands, out from your belly. You'll likely notice time slowing down, your mind getting quieter. When you continue with your day, notice how being more measured and thoughtful changes the emotions in your body and in your interactions.

I offer my clients the opportunity to engage in this practice for several minutes before entering a difficult conversation or meeting. You can even do it in your car for a few minutes before entering a situation that is likely to cause anxiety or an unpleasant reaction of any sort. This practice can be used throughout your days to welcome a calmer, more centered state.

Legal Wisdom

Patience for Your Future

Now that you've had a chance to begin familiarizing yourself with some powerful patience tools, here are applications to develop patience specifically for your divorce process. Don't worry if you haven't mastered or memorized the mantras and postures yet; reread through them when you need to. Much of the divorce process is often in the hands of others. For even the most organized and deliberate, certain aspects of your divorce will seem out of your immediate control. With patience, you can focus your energy and intention on impacting the parts of the process that you *can* control. You can begin to move forward from within. You'll be less likely to require the court's involvement, and you'll make the entire divorce process much more easeful for your family.

Common Points of Reactivity—and How to Manage Them Productively

Now is your time to explore and prepare for the common circumstances that can cause reactivity within yourself and in those around you. Glance through this section to learn a few typical situations in which you might find yourself, and let the stories below help you navigate your own way. After each example, I'll offer a simple mantra to help reframe the experience. If these words don't feel comfortable, replace them with language that's more natural for you. Be sure the statements are specific and positive. When you notice you are feeling impatient, repeat your personal mantra in your mind or aloud several times. This practice will begin to rewire your brain.

Examples of typical situations that can generate unwanted reactivity and consequences are:

* You go to a meeting or court, and your spouse or his lawyer says something patently untrue.

   A common, understandable response is to become enraged. But even if you manage to conceal your rage outwardly, the anger you feel *inside* will interfere with how well you can listen and make choices. Instead, request a pause, leave the room, and go somewhere private where you can raise your arms in power pose and take a few breaths until you feel your inner state change. Go back, take stock of what's going on and what's been said, and if you need to directly address the untruth, make a calm, controlled response. Accept that your partner may have a different internal story.

   During your pause, you may find the lie doesn't actually matter at all. Imagine it leaving the room, dissolving, dissipating. If your spouse or his lawyer behaves this way in a courtroom in the presence of the judge, you won't have the luxury of leaving the room, so do the Breathing for Patience exercise from earlier in this chapter (page 31), and remember that your lawyer should get a chance to respond. And keep in mind that misguided assertions do not define you nor your story. MANTRA: I AM RESPONSIVE, COLLECTED, AND CALM.

* Your child comes home from a night with your ex, and announces that dad/mom's new girlfriend/boyfriend slept over.

Slow yourself down. Remember that your child deserves to have two happy parents, two happy households, two happy places to be, one home. Grab your journal when you can and make a list of your possible responses, but do nothing for at least twenty-four hours. Ask yourself: What response will be most helpful to me and my child? If you have a therapist, talk to him or her prior to responding. MANTRA: THE PRESENT MOMENT IS THE ONLY MOMENT I CAN CONTROL.

* Your lawyer and your ex's lawyer are negotiating, and the tone has turned negative or nasty. You feel ashamed, scared, nervous.

In a calm voice, request a time-out so everybody can calm down. Or tell your lawyer that you'd like to step outside and take a break. On occasion, if your lawyer isn't on the same conscious and compassionate path as you are, be certain to share the work you're doing to create the most optimal environment for your family. MANTRA: I PATIENTLY ALLOW THIS NEGATIVE THOUGHT TO PASS ME BY.

* You hear that your husband is celebrating your soon-to-happen divorce with his new girlfriend by taking an expensive trip, while you're barely making ends meet this month. This trip is clear proof that he can pay more alimony.

Maybe his girlfriend paid for the trip. Maybe his parents did. Maybe it's a business trip. Maybe he rashly charged the trip to his credit card as a way to try to quiet the pain in his own heart. Know that you don't have all the answers, and that this is the perfect time to select a tool for patience and wait to act until you have all the facts. Imagined facts or assumed information mustn't take up your mental space. Once you've carefully considered the alternatives, put them on a shelf in your mind until you have more answers. Chances are that you already have your next meeting scheduled with your lawyer or therapist, so add it to your list of subjects to address, and move on for now. MANTRA: I CAREFULLY CONSIDER ALL POSSIBILITIES.

+ You run into your ex's favorite aunt, of whom you are quite fond. She treats you disrespectfully and makes an offhand derogatory remark in which she blames you for the demise of your relationship.

Divorce is a loss for everyone, and everyone responds to it differently. Instead of being defensive, tell her you care for her and you'll give her space to process what's happening. Maybe even let her know that when the dust settles, you'd like the two of you to pick up where you left off. Wish her well. Make it obvious that you still care. MANTRA: PATIENCE IS MY CHOICE, MY AIM, AND MY JOURNEY.

+ Your ex announces that his new girlfriend will be with him at your child's school play.

As silly as this seems, get scientific. Make a list in your journal of all the polite responses you can offer. Make it aspirational; you don't have to commit to doing or saying anything. Instead of pettiness, plan to act, speak, and interact with others with grace and composure. No need to commit to engaging in small talk, but rehearsing your brave smile is helpful. Most important, your composure will put your child at ease. MANTRA: I PRIORITIZE HAPPINESS IN MY FAMILY.

Examples of Moments When You'll Need Patience with Yourself and Others

In the matters below, you have three ways of responding: defensively, offensively, or elegantly.

Telling your world you're getting a divorce.

Realizing that the indiscretions surrounding your divorce have become publicly known.

Seeing him or her with a new partner in public for the first time.

Going through holidays and other special occasions as a divorced person.

Discovering that your friendships are changing.

Going to meetings with your lawyers or a mediator and hearing your spouse lie or say unpleasant things about you.

In each of these circumstances, your willingness to look at the situation with patience is essential. To consider what others are enduring, particularly your children, is a practice. Even for a few moments, take time to imagine life in others' shoes—how they're seeing, through their lens, with their perception of reality. Suddenly you may find that each person is having a valid experience, and even if it's not true for you, you'll have more space for it all. This practice will help you be more patient, more able to hear what's happening. Use this practice to find the language, the pacing, the voice, and the vision to speak or act in a way that will be heard.

Bring Your Internal Strengths Forward

In your journal, note the events or situations that have created turmoil for you in the past or may cause trouble in the future. Leave
a few lines of space below each one to note how you've previously
been, and then design a new response—a response that in this moment may feel unrealistically aspirational. By engaging in this practice, you will begin to create pathways for new thought. This practice
will help you become aware of such triggers and prep yourself in
advance for the cascade of emotions that may ensue. For each tumultuous trigger, answer each question not with your feelings but solely
with the facts.

How did I deal with this before the divorce/separation?

How am I dealing with this now?

What is the optimal way for me to respond to this?

When the situation comes up again and I didn't offer the optimal
response, what specifically can I do better next time?

Managing Those Moments

Before the fact, prime your system. When you know a potentially
dramatic situation is approaching, prepare your mind. Repeat your
patience mantras. Design positive, compassionate, balanced answers
to questions or topics of conversation that you feel may arise. Aim for
answers that reflect the harmonious state you're striving to maintain.

Both Elena and I find a really effective practice is to have a rule to
send only constructive, proactive responses, particularly in emails.
I encourage my clients to "sleep on it" before sending an email; this

time lag creates space and prevents those heat-of-the-moment discourses that lead to trouble. Elena edits at least two times, including what she wishes to happen—no criticizing, blaming, or shaming. Dissolve your urgent defenses, stop harping on the past, and express what you hope to see in the future.

Everyone has different strengths in interpersonal dynamics, and every relationship is unique. Be patient so you can consider readjusting your expectations. My dear brilliant Grandpa Walter taught me to put people on a shelf rather than throwing them away. As both Elena and I have witnessed, if you choose to make your life a life of practice, you'll become wiser and subtler as the time passes. Relationships are complicated, and even the most acutely painful situations mellow in time, so be patient.

Ask for space. When a situation arises that is bringing on unwanted emotion, find your escape hatch—a break in the dialogue or activity in which you can ask for a moment of space. "Wow, it's been a tough day today. May I have a moment to collect my thoughts?" or even calmly request ten minutes for a "time-out" to organize your thoughts, and to calm and settle your mind.

Step away, take a walk outdoors, head to the restroom. Grant yourself time to take a few breaths and some distance from the conversation or person who seems to be having an impact on your state of mind. Remember that this person is just being him- or herself. It's your choice whether you allow someone to impact or affect you. Bring the most graceful version of yourself back to that conversation, or ask to be excused and to continue at a later time if you feel it's too much for you today.

After a difficult interaction: Laugh, think back, and look forward. No matter how well you handled a trigger, take stock of how it went. Take a quiet moment with yourself. Then carefully and diligently follow the instructions below. Each one will help.

1. Smile. A sense of humor is mandatory right now, and your smile will alter your internal state in a positive direction.

2. Review the spirit of what was said, how you acted. Don't judge yourself, just review. Did you respond or react? If you reacted, replay the ideal design for that scene, the one in which you respond patiently, elegantly. Do it over in your mind so you can do better next time.

3. If you responded with elegance, be proud. Let that impression become the new neutral within you.

DO YOUR BEST. At times, despite your best intentions, patience may have eluded you. Due to some unspeakable slur or misdeed, perhaps you've shouted, cursed, or ranted. Even now, there may be times you just can't help yourself. Pause and practice lengthening your breathing.

NURTURE YOURSELF. It's not easy to be patient when we feel taxed and empty. Patience is possible only when we feel nourished and fulfilled. Take care of yourself with any one or all of these small steps.

EXERCISE. There is no better way to take care of yourself; movement will reset your entire system and make it possible to locate patience in your body and mind. If you don't currently exercise, use your divorce as an excuse to begin your physical makeover. Even a walk every day during which you repeat a relevant mantra either internally or aloud will help you absorb the element you're seeking to embody.

RESIST NUMBING YOURSELF. Drinking, smoking, recreational drugs, gambling, compulsive sex—if you have a vice you've already kicked, divorce is your time to resist and solidify your choice to be clear, clean, and free. As above, exercise is the finest anti-dote to emotional pain; scientifically it's the most efficient way to remove negative emotional energy. A near second best is time with dear friends or counsel from a trusted therapist, teacher, or advisor.

ALLOW YOURSELF TO GRIEVE. There is no shame in the pain you feel. Let the tears flow. Grief is an important part of your healing. Notice the waves of pain; accept them, but don't inhabit the feeling. Let it pass, slowly and with honor.

REDESIGN YOUR INNER DIALOGUE. Review how you talk to yourself, about yourself. What is the tone of the conversation you're having with yourself? Set a timer and spend one minute writing notes to yourself about this. Save this list—we're coming back to it.

For example:

- This divorce is going to ruin me and my family.
- I can't stop sabotaging myself.
- I'm a failure in love. I don't know how to be a good partner or a good parent.
- I feel like a fraud.
- Everyone's judging me.

These patterns of thinking are what we will interrupt here, using a daily practice to reframe your thinking. Those negative thoughts that are arising need to be redesigned and harmonized. This is where radical self-care comes in. Rewire each thought with an I AM statement, as modeled here.

INITIAL REACTION: This divorce is going to ruin me and my family.

TRANSFORMED THOUGHT: *I am committed to being my highest self so this divorce becomes a blessing, a way into a happier, more truthful life for* all *of us.*

INITIAL REACTION: I can't stop sabotaging myself.

TRANSFORMED THOUGHT: *I am deeply appreciative of my body and I'm choosing to care for it.*

INITIAL REACTION: I'm a failure in love. I don't know how to be a good partner or a good parent.

TRANSFORMED THOUGHT: *I* am *love. I am learning to be a steady, stable presence for myself so I can be a steady, stable presence for my future partner and for my family.*

INITIAL REACTION: I feel like a fraud.

TRANSFORMED THOUGHT: *I am a truth-teller. My story is unfolding as an example of an exemplary divorce.*

INITIAL REACTION: Everyone's judging me.

TRANSFORMED THOUGHT: *I am intelligent, caring, capable, and complete. I am free from blame and judgment.*

Take a few moments to tinker with your fears and negative thoughts about yourself, using the examples above. This writing exercise will help you harmonize your misunderstandings about yourself so you can be graceful, kind, present, and patient for this process.

A note about patience, social media, and your electronic communications during your divorce:

I have seen social media and electronic communication via text and email unexpectedly negatively impact many of my clients' divorces. Sara, an outgoing woman in her thirties, couldn't wait for a night out with her best girlfriends to take her mind off of her stressful divorce. It was exactly what Sara needed—an evening of soul-recharging connection, laughing with her dearest friends. The morning after, Sara posted a picture of herself surrounded by her smiling friends. The caption read: "Feeling grateful for the best friends a girl could ever have! Love you all!"

One of those friends liked the picture and commented innocently: "Last night was such fun. Plus you looked gorgeous! I can't wait to see what comes next in your life." Her soon-to-be ex saw that comment and was filled with jealousy-fueled conjecture that spiraled out of control as the days went by. How dare Sara be out having fun and looking hot when he was home alone and on a budget? She probably met a guy at the restaurant. The next time they had a mediation session, there was unnecessary difficulty and delay due to his speculation and anger.

Mindfully managing your online life in the midst of divorce takes patience and thoughtfulness. If you don't have to be on social media for work or monitoring your kids, take a complete break from social media during your divorce process. Let your friends know you'll be readily available by phone, text, and email, and be sure to take the lead by reaching out to them that way.

In addition to potentially causing conflict and hurt, time spent aimlessly scrolling through social media takes away from your capacity to be present. Unless your job requires you to be on social media for longer, limit yourself to three times per day and fifteen minutes at a time; then do something productive.

If you're not on social media for work, curb your use of it until your divorce is final and stay off of it for six months following your final divorce hearing (or longer if you have a particularly contentious divorce). Otherwise adjust all your filters so they are completely private. Even private settings might spark speculation from your ex if he or she can see your posts or your friends' posts on your account through a third-party friend or contact.

Wait twenty-four hours before sending emails or messaging and reread all texts to be sure your content, language, and tone are calm. Only send if you'd be okay with your boss, parent, or child reading those words. Remember that what you're trying to say might be misconstrued. The goal is to patiently dissolve negativity and amplify your objectives. If you have a strong impulse to send a message but are concerned you'll forget it, write it down. If the message is essential, it will be there tomorrow. Patience.

CHAPTER 3

Respect

The Stories We Tell Ourselves

We don't have to agree on anything to be kind to one another.
—UNKNOWN

E ven before it began, Laura had a feeling her marriage would not end well. The casual comment her handsome fiancé had made just two days before their extravagant wedding in the tropics had an edge that she just couldn't shake. She couldn't help but think it was a premonition of things to come, but in her mind, it was too late to cancel. Twenty-two years later, John, now a well-respected, wealthy heart surgeon, announced, "I've outgrown you. I want a divorce."

Laura, who had lived in a state of unrequited love for far too long, was devastated and humiliated. "He didn't even think it was worth talking about." She was stuck in her belief that he always "gets what he wants," as she said through her tears. "He actually told me that I'm not smart enough for him, and he needed more intellectual stimulation from his wife. I gave up my career for him, and when we first got together, I worked to send him through medical school." She told me that she'd given up everything for him, including her career and, as far as she was concerned, a life of her own.

Everything they did and everywhere they went, even just choosing a restaurant, was on John's terms. She was a dutiful wife, caring for his mother, their home, and their boys. "The signs were there that he wanted out years ago, but didn't leave because of the boys," she said. I comforted her. I could feel her pain and shame, but I could also see how she too had made many choices along the way that led to her current predicament. She hadn't respected herself enough to maintain her own individuality, and she'd played roles she'd never intended to play. I helped her understand that she will see whatever she believes—which leads to my next point. She needed to learn to believe in herself in order to see that she'd handed over control of her life. And it was time for her to learn to respect herself enough to create her own new reality.

Developing a Practice of Respect

Self-Respect

When you're on the receiving end of a divorce, self-respect can be eroded easily if you aren't diligently maintaining it. For some, like Laura, it can slip away slowly over time. Living in a marriage filled with emotional strife, disrespectful language, or other forms of neglect and abuse can all contribute to the wearing down of dignity. After passively acquiescing to being trampled on for years by a domineering spouse, self-respect dissolves if we're not paying vigilant attention.

Loss of self-respect isn't limited to those dealing with emotional or physical abuse. Loss of self-respect is a reality of divorce for most people. The reality of impending separation or divorce is disconcerting even to those who initiate the divorce proceedings. Guilt and shame may erode self-respect. "How did I end up like this?" When conflated, divorce can feel confusing and challenging even if it's the best outcome for both parties.

Allow this uncomfortable sensation of imbalance to pass through you, knowing that every insecure and ambiguous feeling you have is absolutely normal, natural, real, and temporary. As you deepen your self-respect, your perspective will shift. Elena describes her own experience in a way that helps clarify this concept at the heart of your present and future happiness.

Elena's Story: What Divorce Taught Me About Self-Respect

Tapping into my own self-respect was a journey of observing countless moments of disrespecting myself, repeatedly. Before I could entertain the reality of seeing myself as worthy of my own or anyone else's respect, I had to see it in my words, my actions, my addictions, my doubts, my fears. We rob ourselves of dignity through the tiniest actions, but we grow self-respect in the same way—with small daily choices to maintain our integrity, tell the truth, and hold ourselves accountable.

We mistake *reference* for *reverence*, looking outside ourselves for validation; we seek external reference points to feel more real. In the throes of your divorce process, build yourself a palace of self-respect within yourself, brick by brick, conversation by conversation, thought by thought. When you find yourself hungry for respect, rather than looking out of yourself, choose to generate one kind thought for yourself, one shift of your innermost attitude toward a more respectful trajectory.

Self-Respect and Your Internal Dialogue

While divorce may not carry the stigma it did thirty or forty years ago, it can still feel shameful, especially when it happens suddenly and unexpectedly. One of my clients was so humiliated when her husband walked out on her that she was afraid to face her parents with the news; she thought they would blame her. Instead, she wrote them a letter and slid it under their front door in the middle of the night.

"My mom showed up the next day on my doorstep with a bouquet of flowers, crying for me, and gave me a hug," she told me later, laughing about the avoidant way in which she'd shared the news with her parents. Even though it seemed that her life was over and she would never feel like herself again, with time she learned how to move past it all, with patience, self-respect, and practice.

Self-respect is elusive. Some of us who lack self-respect lost it so long ago. Finding this awareness is one of those simple understandings that have the power to change your thinking. Elena and I have discussed and confirmed this often during the writing of this book. The stories we tell ourselves have the power to generate our reality if we're not careful. We carry on a subconscious inner dialogue that convinces us that we're not worthy, that we'll never feel tenderness again, never move forward. When you practice becoming aware of your usual internal conversation—the one that keeps you in a state of disrespect for yourself—you'll also have the power to transform it.

Mantras for Self-Respect

Our connection to being the victim is tough to shake. We've all felt stuck, convinced that time's been wasted, that we've been diminished. While it may be a bit unconventional, given my line of work, when I work with people in this kind of state, I ask them to adopt a mantra that I learned from a psychologist many years ago: "I deeply love and accept myself."

Repeat that one simple line aloud to yourself, morning and night, and any other times your inner voice argues otherwise. This may be harder to do than you can imagine. When I get into a discussion with a client about why he or she just cannot say it, it often ends in laughter. If you feel uncomfortable saying this mantra outright, say simply: "I love and accept myself." If that's still too much, warm up with: "I'm working on loving and accepting myself." If you grew up in a home where criticism was the norm or if you were being criticized in your relationship, this will take time and practice. When you're ready, go for it. "I deeply love and accept myself."

Here are other affirmations for self-respect as they pertain to divorce. Choose one that resonates with you, or when you feel inspired to be more specific, write your own. Recite it aloud or to yourself every day as often as possible. Practice makes permanent; your consistency here will rewire your mind so self-respect will become an automatic response within your system.

I am a good person.

There is no limit to what I can accomplish.

I am strong.

I am kind.

I will get through my divorce and be better for it.

I deeply love and respect myself.

Transmitting Respect: Fixed Versus Growth Mindset

According to Stanford University psychologist and motivational expert Carol S. Dweck, PhD, we are guided by one of two mindsets: one is fixed and the other is attuned to growth. In her book *Mindset,* she explains that the fixed mindset is driven by an inner dialogue focused on judging ourselves and others. It's a mindset that views individual capacities and situations as limited. A fixed mindset causes us to avoid challenge, ignore possibility, and feel a sense of powerlessness over any aspect of our future. A fixed mindset says, "It is what it is. And I cannot change it."

With a growth mindset, however, we recognize the potential for evolution within ourselves and our experience. We are able to see our situation as a process of perseverance and learning. A growth mindset stimulates expansion, neurologically and emotionally, enabling us to do the previously unimaginable. A growth mindset says, "Even in this difficult reality I can effectuate change."

Many people come into my office deflated, and, in their fixed mindset, cannot see past this moment; they feel utterly defined by the divorce. Take a moment to consider how you perceive your ability to grow, to transform from this moment. If I were to tell you that today is a clean slate, would it excite you or would you roll your eyes in disbelief?

By way of example, while I'd considered myself to be growth oriented, reading Dweck's book prompted me to see that I wasn't truly turning my thoughts into action. I'd been thinking about writing this book, but I wasn't taking the steps I needed to take in order to bring my vision to life. In what areas in your life could you be more growth oriented? If you feel stuck in any area of your life, here are some ways to move yourself in the direction of growth.

Bring your inner dialogue to the surface. It's time to work in your journal. Pay careful attention to your regrettable actions or negative thoughts and the internal motivation for them. To locate your internal motivation, consider what your mind seems to be "saying" in any given moment of difficulty. Notice if you feel as though you're putting yourself down. Those little moments are based on misunderstandings you've accumulated throughout your life, and they needn't be perpetuated any longer.

It's important to see how the past plays a role in your beliefs today, and how insidiously present the past can be in how you move forward. For example, Elena overworks. She finds herself seeking validation in finishing, accomplishing, and outdoing herself on projects. When we were writing this section, she recalled a teacher of hers who called her ignorant when she was fourteen, a statement that still seems to haunt her and drive her today. Her work is her way to escape, her way to prove that teacher wrong. What's your escape activity? Notice what you may be avoiding and consider why. And consider the negative self-talk that is causing you to limit yourself and make choices to escape—how you run, eat, or otherwise distract yourself in ways that don't serve you. When you become aware of what your critical self is telling you, you'll begin shifting those patterns of behavior because you're shifting how you view yourself. And when you stop doing these activities, what messages or feelings start to come to the surface of your mind? Just notice them without judgment. That's when you can bring the inner dialogue to the surface and shift it.

Elevating Your Self-Respect

ACCENTUATE THE POSITIVES. Once you become an active participant in your life, everything shifts. What is it that brings you joy? Can you begin doing those things and notice that your mood shifts? Rather than passively thinking about the possibilities, take action. Once you begin listening to your inner call to action (no matter how small), you will start feeling better. A ready example is when I hear people worry about where they are going to live post-divorce and yet somehow it all works out in the end. Sometimes we attach to a position so strongly that we disregard the underlying fear. When you find yourself worrying, I encourage you to see those concerns as opportunities to change your mind. What is the precise opposite of that worrisome thought? And as difficult as things may be right now, remember not to take yourself too seriously. It's all going to work out. Where would you *like* to live? What does your dream environment look like and feel like? Accentuate the positives. In this example, if you find you need to move, consider the upsides of forming new friendships, joining a new community, finding new places and faces to explore.

ACT THE WAY YOU WANT TO FEEL. The best way to release critical inner dialogue is to use small actions to drive the way you want to feel. Do what lifts your spirits, and notice when you're about to choose nonessential activities that bring you down. For example, if romantic comedies have you crying instead of laughing, stop watching them for now. Find the activities that bring you joy, even for thirty minutes a day, just for yourself. If you love going to the movies, replace romantic comedies with romance-neutral mysteries. Or skip watching movies altogether and go hiking with a neighbor or friend. Even little things can give you a lift.

WRITE DOWN EVERYTHING THAT GIVES YOU A LIFT AND BRINGS YOU JOY. If you feel more down than joyful, note when you feel okay. Many feel that offering your services to help others nurtures the spirit: volunteer at a soup kitchen, care for animals at an animal shelter, visit a needy elderly relative or friend. If nothing here seems to work, be brave and seek some professional assistance in helping you to smooth out the edges. Create a section in your journal where you jot down the happy moments. Over time this list will grow and can serve as a centering point of reference for you when you need a boost.

SMILE OFTEN AND EVERY DAY. I'm most at home when I'm smiling. Smiling brings positive energy no matter what the moment is bringing. I used to have a placard on my desk that read "Keep smiling, it makes people wonder what you've been up to." Smiling helps melt anxiety and invites empathetic connection. Make it a point to greet at least one person every day with a smile, especially when you don't feel like it. This is one small action you can take to definitively shift your inner state.

LOOK IN THE MIRROR AND SEE YOUR HUMANITY. Many of us were taught that being "emotional" is a sign of weakness or failure. In my personal experience, a lot of emotionality felt out of control to me when I was younger, but now I see another side. I held so much of my own sadness and frustration inside that I had headaches. Now that I let myself cry sometimes, I feel more capable of letting emotions pass through rather than accrue and stagnate in my body.

So often I hear about the sadness, shame, and disappointment of divorce. I wish I could introduce every person who feels this way to every other person so they could see that they're never alone. Although everyone processes divorce differently, there's a universality to your feeling deeply. There's nothing wrong with you for expressing your emotions, within reason. At some point, most who divorce can eventually look back and see it as a fortunate experience. It may not feel that way now, but most likely it will.

SURROUND YOURSELF WITH THOSE WHO NOURISH YOU. Dweck writes that people with a fixed mindset tend to seek out people who are worse off than they are so they can feel better about themselves. Instead, I dare you to surround yourself with others who lift your soul, those who help you move forward and flourish. In your journal, list your friends, colleagues, relatives, and other people with whom you interact on a frequent basis. Next to each name, write down one word that indicates how this person has influenced your life. Surround yourself only with those who help you respect yourself and others—those who help you be the person you want to be.

END THE BLAME AND MOVE FORWARD GRACEFULLY. Nobody is served in the blame game. Take ownership of your life, starting now. Owning your part is a reflection of fearless evolution, and eventually it feels great. There's no sense in dwelling on the past, because this wears you down and holds you back from moving on. Recognize that choices were made based on what you knew and who you were at the time. Now, years later, you may find it easy to say that you made the wrong choice, but you didn't know it was wrong then. It's certainly easier to blame your ex than to acknowledge that you were a participant. Accepting your part in creating your path is essential in order to move forward. To move forward gracefully, deliver your apologies and/or let go of blame and move on. Set the example. Energize your future, and remind yourself every day that you are in control of your destiny.

Commit to New Possibilities

When you're feeling especially stuck, make a list of five categories of your life.

Friendship/Family Relationships

Kids

Romance

Career

Community

Beneath each category, write a list of your wishes. How do you want your friendships to feel? How will they help you and you them? How can your kids be the healthiest and happiest? What does your ideal romance look and feel like? What role will this new person take in your life, with both you and your kids? What is your ideal career, and how do you see yourself in that role? Do you feel connected to your community? How could you be more deeply engaged? Each time you go back into your list, refine your vision. Over time this one writing practice will breathe life into your new existence; your writing will give shape to your highest thoughts. Keep this ongoing list close at hand, and it will change your life.

Movement and Posture for Self-Respect

To cultivate self-respect, sit or stand tall and own your space and your stance. Separate your feet about hip-width apart.

Lengthen your toes, and feel your feet on the floor or the ground. Place your left hand on your heart center and feel yourself present there. As your breathing deepens, the sensation of presence in your heart grows. Continue to take deep breaths until you feel self-respect rising inside, guiding your spine to lengthen taller.

Breathing for Respect

Take a seat or lie down (but stay awake) and breathe. Take this time to simply lengthen your breathing, making your inhalation and exhalation as long as possible. When you lengthen your inhalation, invite a quiet sense of clarity. When you lengthen your exhalation, invite a sense of grounded, abiding respect for yourself and for the world around you. Simply lengthening your breathing has more palpable benefits—your cells receive more nourishment and your immune function is enhanced.

Meditation for Respect

Elena offers this quick shift of vantage point to remind herself and her students to connect to the bigger picture. Enjoy these moments of connection, as a deepening of respect for yourself and the world around you.

Take a seat, preferably outdoors or in sight of the natural world. Place your fingertips next to your hips on the floor or preferably on the grass or the ground, and reach into the earth, creating the shape of a mountain with your arms.

This grounds you, creating a sense of stability and a deep connection with the earth. As we deepen our awareness of the earth and our place here, we naturally inhabit our bodies more completely, allowing feelings of security, respect, and, most important, self-respect to take shape. Take five resonant breaths there, in connection with the earth, and use the earth as your reference point to remind you of the miracle of your own existence and experience here. Then bring your hands to your thighs and continue to breathe slowly for as long as twenty minutes. Let this sitting grant you perspective, and a return to a remembrance.

Legal Wisdom

Respecting Your Spouse and Designing Your Future

Even if feeling true respect is a challenge, such as in incidences of infidelity, abuse, lying, trauma, or even criminal behavior, you can still act respectfully. There's a world of difference. My father taught me this lesson when I was ten, not too long after he and my mother divorced. I felt sad and angry. I remember saying, "I don't respect you." He bent down, looked me squarely in the eyes, and firmly told me, "You don't have to respect me, but you have to be respectful to me." I got it. In time I came to understand that we all have faults. Some are more obvious than others, but sometimes those you judge for being utterly different from you are fascinating, inspiring characters worthy of compassion and care. Often those with the most obvious flaws possess a strength and depth obscured by our disappointment, especially when we focus on their difficult or negative personality characteristic(s). We all have different triggers and standards, so we can't judge anyone according to our subjective understanding. People and relationships are complicated; if you seek fault, you'll find it, and if you seek respect, you'll find that, too.

Now here's the hard part. You might be separating from a person who doesn't tell the truth. Liars lie, then twist the story more and turn it against their perceived adversary. I've seen my fair share of cases where lies are told outright, even in court—and sometimes even the judge believes the liar. Those who lie and mishandle their lives are often notoriously loose cannons in the divorce process. They have a tendency to create a more litigious, reactive environment. They interrupt, argue, and put everyone on edge, which can make respect the ultimate challenge. Here's how to keep your cool.

Attend to What Matters Most

Respect is a practice. Rising above the lies, developing clear boundaries, and allowing things to bounce off you are essential skills in your divorce process. Find the traces of good amid the lies; remember, people are multifaceted. I've seen impressive liars be incredible parents. People who lie often may not realize that they're lying. In fact, there are mental disturbances that cause people to lie incessantly and unwittingly. When you remove the notion that the lie is malicious or personal, tensions may start to lift. And if you can't find the good, find the neutral. As Elena notes, "Find that neutral place where you're holding little to no tension in your body with any of it."

If you can't even find that, start by just acting respectfully. When you show respect to your ex or soon-to-be ex, you'll notice that tensions ease. Particularly when you are in the presence of your children, your respectful behavior teaches them volumes about how to be a functioning, capable, adaptable person. Their lives and yours will slowly become more settled—and the divorce process more civil—when you're respectful. When you show respect toward your spouse and his or her lawyer, you'll be more likely to get some semblance of respect in return. Let's look at it this way.

In most cases, when you got married, you and your spouse had mutual respect for each other, and shared love, affection, and admiration. As you exit your formal relationship, show as much respect as possible. Even if you are gravely disappointed in your ex's choices, even if you've been profoundly hurt by certain behaviors, you can locate at least one admirable trait or worthy facet of your former partner's presence in your life. To begin cultivating respect, focus on seeing that aspect.

Taking a step back from your position to cultivate respect helps you slow down and recognize the limited awareness that's led to this moment. Especially if you have been betrayed or have had your heart broken, that respect will help you move forward with more kindness and enable you to set a better example for your family. Remember, from an emotional perspective, you and your ex are on different timelines. When I first became a divorce lawyer, an elder colleague brilliantly once said to me, "Gabrielle, divorce is like a fine wine; it needs time to age well." Below I'll offer a few more ways to help you move respect ahead easefully.

Mantras to Respect the Other

The following are examples of affirmations for displaying respect while going through your divorce and during the times you must interact with your ex after the divorce. Choose one that resonates with you or write your own. Recite it aloud or to yourself every day as often as possible, but at least in the morning after you wake up and before going to bed at night. Granted, this may be hard to do, but remember, it's to benefit you and your kids.

1. My children and I matter above all else.

2. Harmony serves us better than discord.

3. Nobody is all good or all bad. I commit to finding the highest intentions within my ex.

Meditation to Respect the Other

Elena had a profound shift in her understanding early on, before her divorce was finalized. She had an opportunity to shift everything she assumed true about divorce. Her story helps clarify a critical aspect of co-parenting through divorce, and the meditation she offers will help you efficiently locate a respectful stance.

> To locate respect for my son's father was perhaps the most important mission throughout our separation and divorce process. I'll never forget one particular conversation that I had with Lauren Zander, cofounder of the life coaching company Handel Group and author of *Maybe It's You*. She stared deeply into my eyes at our second meeting and told me that my son's present happiness and future well-being depended on the way in which I love his dad—not romantically, but as my family, forever.
>
> She taught me that my son's future relationships hinge on how well I honor and show respect for his father. This was

not immediately obvious to me, and it took a long time to make this happen; first within me and then with him. I was angry, unwilling, untrusting, and untrustworthy. I didn't feel seen or heard, and sabotaged the process enough to know that this was a huge hurdle for us both.

But that one conversation with Lauren gave me the biggest piece of the puzzle. You don't need to agree or feel romantically connected to find respect. One of you needs to consistently cultivate an overarching reverence for the time you did spend together, in honor of your own future and that of your children. Even if your ex resists this teaching, by practicing respect, you can change the tone of your future, one conversation, one thought at a time.

The path informed by this intention has been one of deepening friendship and loyalty, but it took us time to learn to trust each other again, and to find a true love that transcends the initial sting of divorce. We now see that our journey was the most perfect possible route for us to take, to find our current partners, to realize the depth of our present friendship, and to see our boy thriving with abundant support and love.

Writing Your Respect

First, note and write down when you feel respected, hopefully even with regard to your spouse. Consider what moments of your day feel full of respect, and note why. Even if it's two minutes in the quiet of the morning, write down what adds to any sensation of respect and what you're bringing to that moment. Note moments of self-respect, and note moments when you feel others are respecting you. A focus on seeing respect will help you untangle the emotional web that will interfere with the elegant navigation of your divorce. And if you have children, it will be invaluable for them to see your example of how to bring respect and even to respectfully disagree. Now taking deep belly breaths, re-read this list and take it into your body. When you feel a shift inside, move on.

Reinforcing your higher self through written expression will help you inch your way toward the self-perception that will move you forward in a more positive direction.

Transform Your Dynamic

SHIFT INTO NEUTRAL. You loved your partner once, but now you can feel only disgust. Recall the moment you met, the places you went, the romance, the connection. Somewhere in the middle, where the present reality meets the past, is neutral ground. Shift into neutral, where you'll slowly practice holding less tension in your body, and continue orienting yourself more positively toward the future.

IMAGINE THE TWO OF YOU GETTING ALONG. Elena suggests you gather the internal understandings you're learning in this book and envision the two of you getting along despite what's happened, letting all the negatives flow away like water under a bridge. This will not happen immediately, but if you are clear in your vision of respect, it will materialize. When you can stop admonishing yourself for decisions you've made (or have failed to make) and can start to forgive his or her actions, you will be able to respect both yourself and your ex, and move forward with some semblance of peace.

GENERATE A LIST OR A VISION BOARD TO ENVISION WHAT'S COMING. You found love and respect once, and more awaits you. Make a list or vision board with words or images of the things that you respect or admire about yourself and your ideal relationship. Let positive sensations and imagery in, and keep this board or list near to your heart. Let it be your guide as you enter any meeting, court appearance, or mediation session. When you keep respect at the center of your awareness, you will guide your life forward gracefully.

WORK THE EDGES. Write down what you respect about your ex or soon-to-be ex. If you have a spouse who is an addict or an abuser, finding a place for respect in your heart may be especially challenging. But it is definitely a possibility. The way to go about it is to do what I call working the edges—that is, finding his or her redeeming qualities and putting your focus there. See him or her through a different lens. With safety concerns, create a parenting plan with safeguards for your children. Recall when you were married, especially at the beginning, you saw plenty of good in your spouse. Maybe she or he made you laugh, surprised you on your birthday, worked hard so the two of you could buy your first house. Maybe at first you enjoyed these signs of love, but later such actions didn't mean as much, perhaps because you realized this was just not your person.

Perhaps you'll need to note this in the past tense—as in, what you've respected about him or her in the past. This seems elementary, but it will energize you and help you heal. Keep this list close by and add to it as things occur to you.

KEEP THE FOCUS ON YOU AND YOUR KIDS. Remember to focus on what you need rather than on how your spouse is acting; you may feel like you're talking to a wall. Focusing on the ongoing painful events rather than the goal doesn't accomplish anything. Observe without evaluating. Respond rather than react.

This is of the utmost importance. Respect is absolutely essential to the mental health of you and your children. And when you are displaying and showing respect, the other person will find it harder to put you down.

ACCEPT YOUR HUMANNESS. Nobody makes a perfect choice. Finding true respect for the person who betrayed you requires that you process the grief of the loss. Saying so is not going to make it happen. Everything unfolds over time. Even getting to neutral is not going to happen overnight. Allow time to heal.

CHAPTER 4

Clarity

So You Can Perceive What Else Is Possible

In the light of calm and steady self-awareness, inner energies wake up and work miracles without any effort on your part.

—SRI NISARGADATTA MAHARAJ

Y our cultivation of clarity increases the likelihood that you'll activate the healing and ease you seek for yourself and your family. When you direct your attention on specific aims, you create subconscious openings for those actions and results. This chapter is about becoming clear and maintaining a focused mind. You'll create lists of objectives, learn how to separate needs from wants, and prioritize the facts rather than your emotions as much as possible. This is not about neglecting your feelings; the idea is to maintain a steady, focused mind so you can reach agreement and create comfort for all involved, as efficiently and effectively as possible.

When you're flooded with emotion, you will find it particularly difficult to think clearly. To illustrate this point, make a fist with your thumb turned inward, and the other four fingers draped over the thumb. Your thumb represents your instinctive, animal brain, and the other four fingers are your rational mind. When you lose your cool or "blow your top," those four fingers figuratively lift up, leaving your fearful animal brain in an unprotected swirl of chaos, with little space for clarity. When you engage your rational mind, those four fingers cover your reactive instinctive brain, your instincts are metaphorically and literally blanketed or quieted, and the chaos is stilled. At that point, you can defer to your clear-minded, insightful intuition. So let's sort through some practical ways to help you get clear.

Lists Beget Clarity

By now you may have noticed that I love making lists. These help me accomplish my missions day to day, year to year. Lists bring me clarity. As a kid, I had lists for every holiday, organizing my thoughts to ask for what I wanted. As I got older, I made lists to remind myself of the qualities I sought in a partner and the lessons I had learned from each relationship. When I was in college, I walked through a hip apartment in a convenient, desirable neighborhood (both important to me), imagining myself living in this one particular space that caught my eye. I wrote it down, and while I was away on a semester abroad one year later, a friend at college asked me if I might be interested in sharing an apartment the following semester. It was the exact same apartment I had on my list.

In the last twenty years, my lists have been more focused on my family, my relationships, my household. And I've also kept meticulous lists of the points I want my clients to remember at certain stages of their divorce process, and, of course, the elements of a graceful, elegant divorce. The lists are ever changing, and they've become templates for how I've lived and produced my best work.

Making lists is a discipline that enables you to clarify your thoughts, make them specific, and then create the realities. Your words have real power; when you see what you've written, you can shift the way you act and create habits to change the way you see and lead your life. Lists will help you put your life in order and envision your future. My aim here is to help you shift the focus of your divorce process away from sadness or anger, and find ways to clearly see the potential you have to make your life even better apart.

Be Specific

Specificity is key. If I'm vague about what I want—such as "I'd like to write a book someday"—it's unlikely to happen. But when I'm clear in my vision and write about it specifically as if it's happening now—"I'm writing a conversation-changing book on how to separate with elegance"—and list the specific ways to make it happen, it materializes. Notice your opportunities and take small steps in the direction you visualize. When I drilled down on the essential elements of the process, the outline for the book became clear and took shape naturally.

It's not enough to have a vague goal; clarity is key. Visualize what you want and write it in the present tense, as if it's happening right now. In the next paragraph, notice the difference below between the first, vague statement and the second, a specific plan that involves caring, concern, and creativity.

"I'm happy, my family is happy." That's vague and less likely to materialize than a more specific statement such as:

"I take the steps each week to help my family feel at ease with my separation and divorce. I stay in touch with my child's father, communicating with him every other day with updates when I have the kids. I am kind to his parents, sending them photos and keeping them in the loop." With such specific objectives, you set the stage to make this ease a reality for your family.

Creating goals and listing the actions needed to reach them will attract the resources, energies, and people to help you shift your trajectory. This process will enable you to focus your mind, generate clear intentions, clarify the issues in your divorce, and prioritize them. You can bring your intentions into your new reality. The process of moving from wanting something to making it happen, from desire to creation, involves three simple steps, which you'll explore in more depth after you begin cultivating more positivity.

VISUALIZE—What do you want, where do you want to go? State it in the present tense, as specifically as possible.

INTERNALIZE—List the actions it will take to feel it and embrace it as true. Bring your attention to your goal through a list of actions.

REALIZE—Allow yourself to feel your forward movement by keeping a journal or a list of how your actions have yielded results.

Mantras for Clarity

When creating the conditions for your divorce, you need to keep clear, positive thoughts and statements close at hand so you can cultivate clarity throughout your process. Listed below are some possibilities for a mantra or affirmation to help you move through this process of generating more positivity in your being.

Choose one of the statements below that resonates with you or write your own. Recite it aloud or to yourself every day as often as possible. Try this for one week in the morning after you wake up and before going to bed at night.

My mind is strong.

My thoughts are clear.

My thoughts and actions are positive and caring.

My vision for kindness and clarity moves us all forward.

Movements for Clarity

For Elena, clarity is about cultivating connection with your navel center, your center of power, which requires both breathing and gentle awareness of how you move.

Take a moment either seated or standing to place one hand on your navel and breathe deeply into your hand, inflating your belly and creating more space. As you exhale, let your navel move back, toward your spine, and connect to your innermost strength. Taking even five to ten breaths like this can significantly shift your state from confused to clear.

Then as you inhale, lift your arms and inflate your belly. As you exhale, return your hands to your heart and welcome your navel back toward your spine. Take five to ten breaths with the arm movements, and you've just invited in a new sense of uplifted, clear focus.

Visualize and Internalize

Be Positive and Stay Positive

Keep your focus on positive, forward movement in order to dispel negativity and keep it out of your mind. Don't give voice to what you don't want; that keeps negativity in your sphere. In order to manifest what you *do* want, state your intentions clearly and list the actions needed to accomplish them deliberately. Here are some examples of aims for your divorce, with actions you'd take to reach those goals:

Peaceful interactions with your ex

Financial security

Happy kids

Settled in your sweet new life

Positive, loving, supportive relationship (romance/love)

Now, under each, list some potential actions to take to accomplish each intention.

Peaceful interactions with your ex

Take time to listen during conversations, meditations, and meetings.

Be consciously kind to him/her during drop-off and pickup.

Organize custody in a caring, creative manner to ensure everyone's comfort.

Financial security

Consider hiring a financial planner or consultant.

Review all accounts and cash flow patiently and slowly.

Create a budget that is broken down into the smallest bits—daily, weekly, monthly, annually.

Happy kids

Consider hiring a parenting coordinator, or consult with someone who's been on this path and successfully cleared the path for divorcing with kindness.

When you have them, do a nightly check-in with kids at bedtime.

Ask yourself *and* your kids what you can improve, and how you can meet their needs more efficiently and efficaciously.

Settled in your sweet new life

Take time for self-care each week/month, including time off for healing treatments.

Create space for reflection and meditation.

Make a special effort to forge friendships that honor past, present, and future.

Let's look at how to manage when you have an ex who truly isn't cooperating, who's behaving poorly, with whom it seems impossible to reach agreements rationally. In that case, your intention or aim might simply be to dissolve your own reactivity, with the needed actions below to give you clarity on how to proceed on a moment-to-moment basis.

Dissolve reactivity.

Limit exposure.

Breathe deeply while with him/her.

Always pause prior to replying.

Design efficient conversations to be had in safe public places, outlining points in advance.

Plan for your own measured responsiveness for unanticipated interactions.

Positive, loving, supportive relationship

You may feel ambivalent about entering a new relationship—that's perfectly natural.

When you're ready, you may find great joy in exploring possibilities for a new, positive relationship to unfold. Get clear and specific.

Consider what qualities bring you joy or contentment.

Examine your inner desires for companionship or love.

Cultivate list of desirable traits.

Make space for and remain open to love.

Realize

Explorations for Your Future

Here are a few of the most important considerations to keep your divorce clear and more easeful. Under each category, you may write in sentences or simply list words that remind you of your internalized vision realized. Remember to keep your words present tense, precise, and positive.

COMMUNICATION REGARDING THE CHILDREN. Your kids may live between two households, but they need clear, consistent boundaries. This is especially true when younger children are involved. Their sense of their place in the world begins with family and consistency. If you and your ex have a difficult time agreeing, have your aims clearly set in your mind, but remain flexible. Clear vision and clear communication are your top priorities.

YOUR NEW HOUSEHOLD. You may or may not be moving to a different house, but your post-separation and/or post-divorce environment will be brand-new. Begin to devise what your household might look like. Make your list: visualize, internalize, and realize. The division of money and material assets in a divorce can be a contentious and trying process. You'll begin that process in earnest in chapter 8.

YOUR SELF-CARE. Taking care of yourself at this time in your life is crucial in keeping you grounded and focused. In the beginning, your healing time might be as simple as remembering to eat; later it can be a monthly massage or daily meditation; any nourishment you grant yourself will serve your entire family. Actively engaging in thoughtful self-care may be the most selfless thing you do in terms of improving your relationship and becoming more present for yourself and for your family. When you're happy, your kids will adjust to their new situation.

HELPING YOUR EX. While you cannot change your ex's behavior or what's happened between you, you can rise above it and model clear, kind communication. For example, if your ex lacks organizational skills and you have joint custody of your kids, you can offer to take on the school forms, packing for camp, or scheduling the week's activities; then suggest that your ex takes them for other activities for which (s)he's well suited.

YOUR KIDS' RESPONSIBILITIES. Instead of complaining about how much more work there is to do as the only adult in the house, give your kids meaningful tasks. Most kids can do more than we expect of them. Begin by creating a list of daily tasks that need to be done— prepping dinner, making beds, emptying lunch boxes. Have them compose their own lists, too; they might surprise you with their helpfulness. Divide the responsibilities, be clear on expectations, and get creative to make it interesting.

Be thoughtful with your lists so you'll be able to address your divorce productively and clearly. Review them, check in with them each month, and make sure they're still relevant. Your lists will become your guides to a well-designed divorce.

Why is this seemingly simple quality of clarity so critical in the divorce process? For most of us, being clearheaded while processing extreme emotion is virtually impossible. In order to have clarity, you have to either suspend or dispel strong emotion. Your lists are there to catch you when emotion seems to take over.

For Elena, clarity is both an aim and a practice.

Clarity is both my direction and my best habit. Rediscovering my identity outside my role as a wife was both frightening and profoundly liberating. During that journey I realized that clarity was crucial.

What does clarity look like? For me, clarity is seeing the top priority in any moment (kids' ease, peace for all of us, a quiet moment to myself) so I can let go of what blocks us from kindness. Clarity is knowing that nothing is personal. If I had not had some semblance of clarity, my divorce process could have been contentious; instead, it was peaceful and even pleasant at times. Early on in the process, clarity within myself was most important for our entire family's process. When I wasn't clear, we all felt it. When I was in my addiction, we all knew it. Without my clarity, nobody else could function optimally. It was as though I held the key to the ecology of our household. Remember, if you're reading these words, so do you.

What does clarity feel like? Clarity reveals itself in the form of a calm, steady body that comes from paying attention, communicating well, and surrounding yourself with the support of good friends. With clarity, you're asking the right questions and granting yourself healthy doses of silence.

When I'm clear, I'm telling the truth, granting others their space, and knowing nothing is personal. I'm reliable, prompt, neat, organized, and able to release what isn't serving me. When I'm clear, I'm able to offer my family the best that I can be.

Healthy Grieving Is a Path to Clarity

Divorce is almost always accompanied with a sense of loss. Even if you know that divorce was the wisest choice, consider Elisabeth

Kübler-Ross's five stages of grief. While these stages are classically associated with the death of a loved one, there is wisdom in contextualizing the loss of your relationship similarly, on your path to more clarity.

DENIAL—Refusal to accept that the marriage or relationship is over. This can cause us to pursue more attention and forgiveness.

ANGER—Anger can cause us to cast blame on the other or blame ourselves.

BARGAINING—This can cause us to try to "repair" the relationship by blindly promising to change.

DEPRESSION—Depression can set in when we realize that the marriage or relationship is truly finished. When we are depressed, it seems that the book on love is closed. We've not yet realized that a new chapter is beginning.

ACCEPTANCE—This is the most important stage. Acceptance is the moment we realize that the page is turning, potential is brewing, and consistent clarity is forthcoming.

Grief is real. Crying and clearing the strongest emotions from your body are necessary, both physically and mentally. Exercise and hydration are crucial to keeping your body well and allowing the grief to move efficiently through. Get clear on your nutrition, your activities, and your creativity so you can experience your feelings but not be a slave to them. Adding movement to your routine will keep the current of creativity moving through your body and mind. Exercise in any form will help you choose courage, engage in activities that serve you, and release your grief so you can move into a new phase of your life.

Elena's Thoughts on Forgiving Yourself as Healthy Grieving

The American poet Buddy Wakefield once said, "Forgiveness is the release of all hope for a better past." More important, are you able to forgive yourself? Can you officially excuse yourself for your dashed hopes? Instead, can you see this as a pivotal moment in which the clouds are clearing and your priorities are shifting? This idea of what could have been or what should have been acts like a blockade, keeping the situation from evolving and you from fully flourishing. Recognize your grief. Make room for the release and welcome in what's slowly unfolding.

How? In meditation, we recognize what's present in this moment, releasing judgments and undoing the difficulty. As humans, we readily develop and give life to the most fundamental misunderstandings within our minds, and this meditation helps unravel those misperceptions so we can move forward with clarity.

Mindful breathing is one of the simplest ways to remember this. For the next few moments, as you breathe in, silently say to yourself, "Breathing in, I calm my body." Then as you exhale, silently say to yourself, "Breathing out, I smile." Then, "Breathing in, I invite a new reality." Finish with, "Breathing out, I release any misunderstanding."

"Breathing in, I calm my body."

"Breathing out, I smile."

"Breathing in, I invite a new reality."

"Breathing out, I release any misunderstanding."

In a few short breaths, this practice helps us realize that

we are suffering due to our misunderstanding of what's happening, and it helps us see that others are also suffering, causing them to act in the ways that they do. When we are able to clearly and calmly perceive this suffering that we're all experiencing, we're able to release judgments, develop compassion, and relax our hold on anger, fear, and sadness. These few breaths offer motivation to move forward and will also transform the environment in which you live.

Legal Wisdom for Clarity

Clarity helps you dissolve the assorted emotions that can make your divorce process seem overwhelming. Practicing clarity invites you to see your divorce and all its facets honestly, without ignoring what scares you and without judging yourself or anyone else. This opens the door to productive communication and confident decision-making—for all involved. Practicing clarity will enable you to cease dramatizing and keep your priorities in order.

In my experience at the negotiating table, clarity is contagious. When my client and I exhibit reflective listening, thereby demonstrating that we've heard the other party's side, everyone feels more easeful, because the other side is feeling truly heard and considered. Clarity might even move you to take responsibility for aspects of your separation you'd never dreamed of owning, which can pave the way for a faster, easier resolution. When you're clear, the conversation can flow in a meaningful and forward-moving direction.

Wants Versus Needs: Clarity in the Material World

You may not even like the silver flatware given to you as a wedding present by your aunt. But when your spouse lays claim to it in your separation process, it might seem a lot more important. Clarity will help you determine if you really need the tea set or just want it because (s)he wants it.

Clarity within the context of asset division is the ability to delineate what you need from your past life to get on in your new life, and what you want or desire to take with you. This kind of challenge goes on all the time in divorces, and wastes your time and money. When you're wrapped up in the emotional struggle, a good dose of clarity can help your decision-making, and can enable you to walk away from such wasteful, draining arguments.

Wants or desires are very powerful and may *seem* like needs: I need the house and all the furniture; I need full custody; I need the minivan.

In many cases, these perceived needs reflect an underlying fear: If I can't keep the house, I won't ever have a proper home again. If I don't have the minivan, I won't be able to transport my children.

Recognizing that emotion clouds decision-making is essential. It can be extremely helpful to work out such questions from a point of clarity, factually, sometimes via email rather than by phone to keep the emotions out of the discourse.

The idea is to consider how to give in order to receive what you really need—a regular schedule that benefits the children, a fair split of the assets, a weekly or monthly family meeting.

When one party gives a little, the other party will (in most cases) do the same. Make a list of your needs and wants, and know the difference so you can reach a resolution in your process with greater fluidity, less emotional drama, and fewer unnecessary expenses and litigious actions. Let's give this a try by making a list of a different sort.

Asset division is always complicated and potentially contentious. Here we'll just touch upon how to organize your own thoughts clearly to facilitate your asset division. In chapter 8 we will discuss this issue further.

For now, though, think clearly about your wants and needs. Make a simple two-column list and begin writing. Now that the considerations of patience and respect have been introduced as concrete aims in your process, this list might look a bit different than it would've looked when you first began reading this book.

Needs are what is right and best for each party. A need is determined in accordance with your version of the facts, as impersonally and objectively as possible.

Wants are based on emotion, desire, and past experience. They are by definition personal and subjective.

Elena suggests that you spend time with this list as often as you can, taking into consideration your continually evolving mood and understanding of your ex, your children, and your future. She offers: "Take only what you truly need. Greediness in this context is detrimental to yourself, your kids, and any future amicable relationship with your ex. Give what you can, and take just what you need. That practice has helped my family over the years in creating a feeling of abundance, generosity, and sharing that has helped our son feel settled and learn what it means to choose magnanimity over selfishness."

Writing to Clarify and Create Your New Reality

One crucial concept has informed both Elena's and my path regarding a good divorce. You can, you will, you *must* envision and manifest your new reality. Get clear about what makes you feel most alive, then imagine that uplifted sensation. Really experience it. Store that feeling in your body and your mind. Map out your vision of what you want your post-divorce life to look like, make your list of specific aims, and note actions needed to make each so.

To help you in your process, here's an example. A few years ago, my husband was complaining that our home was too small, yet we couldn't afford to move at that time. One day, I suggested that he make a list of the attributes of our dream home, and he indulged me.

M's Dream Home

Fireplace

Entry space

Mudroom attached to garage

Screened-in porch

Open living space

Open kitchen

Four bedrooms

Finished basement with guest room

Gym

Huge backyard

Although we'd been casually looking for another house since the day we moved into that current house, nothing better had materialized. A short time later, I ran into a friend with our two little boys in tow, pregnant with our third. As we got to talking, I told her we needed more space. She promptly pointed to my stomach, smiling, and said, "Buy my house!"

I rattled off M's dream home list and she laughed because I almost exactly described her home. Although the house was slightly outside our projected budget, with clarity as my imperative I set a viable financial goal and created the conditions that allowed my vision to be realized seemingly effortlessly. I factored in a few more billable hours to reach my goal. Then in the hours I was with my boys and not working, I committed to being more present with them.

After all that planning, what actually happened, as if by magic, was that an unexpected settlement came in on a long-forgotten file. I earned just exactly what we needed to close the deal. I never had to change my schedule after all. I truly believe that all my clear internalized vision and energy around earning more money created conditions for success. In the following month, we signed the contract on the house, and we've been living there ever since. It didn't have the gym M wanted, but the sellers left behind the very gym equipment M would have wanted in a personal gym. Coincidence? Maybe. Clarity? Yes.

Create Healthy Habits

Your life is comprised of the patterns you practice in your thinking and in your actions. You can actually shift how you think by choosing one modification of your habits, to cultivate more clarity in every aspect of our experience. Little by little, we can change by creating healthy habits and choosing clarity over chaos on a consistent basis.

We lose clarity when we take things personally. So often in divorce cases I've managed, when one side personalizes the actions of the other side, it slows the process down, muddying the waters. Nothing is truly personal. When both sides get in the habit of sticking to the facts and keeping their minds focused on what's needed, momentum is gained and the process of resolution is smoother.

"Habits make change possible," writes happiness expert Gretchen Rubin in *Better Than Before*. As we repeat the same ritual, thought, or action, time after time, it becomes automatic. We no longer have to think about it and, voilà, a new habit has been created. You truly have the power to re-create your life by establishing new ways of thinking. Of being. Little by little you can truly shift your life from the inside out. But to do this, you need to be clear.

As you've already practiced, get clear on what you want in your life moving forward and on what you can release from the past. Begin to release your attachment to past habits that no longer serve you and begin cultivating the new habits you will need to bring your vision to fruition. With consistency over time, your new habits will become automatic. Seemingly effortlessly, you will shift your state of being and your life.

Accept What You Cannot Change

Acceptance is born of clarity and will help you move beyond the mindset of wishing things were different. Albert Einstein supposedly defined insanity as "doing the same thing over and over again and expecting different results." When you're clear, you'll expect that your spouse will continue to be who (s)he is—and you'll carefully manage that reality, releasing your expectations and building a new way of relating. These adjustments to your expectations and your behavior will help you feel freer and happier. Your relationship dynamic will then begin to shift, so both of you can feel more at ease within yourselves and within the new form of your relationship.

Recognize and acknowledge that those living with undiagnosed, untreated mental disabilities and addictions need particular care. I've counseled my clients to create systems to work around these situations, and to remember that nothing is personal.

Rewrite Your Story

Accepting what you cannot change is an essential practice for clarity, helping you to move forward in creating your new reality. Rewriting your story—literally and figuratively—is like rewiring your brain to become habituated to new possibilities so that these positive thoughts become automatic. You're creating a practice of redesigning your thoughts each day, so that typically negative thought patterns can be transformed into more positive, productive, proactive thoughts and behaviors. Acknowledging that these are all first-world, minor issues in the grand scheme of events. But your attitude on a moment-to-moment basis *does* have an impact on how you feel as well as on your entire family's emotional well-being, so take the time to address these small annoyances (that admittedly often feel huge) in a concretely positive way.

Here are some examples.

(S)HE'S NEVER ON TIME.

TRANSFORMED: *I know it's hard for her/him to be punctual, so I'll build in extra time to accommodate for their timing. The kids will see and feel my flexibility and kindness, and they will learn from that. (Elena and I both took a long time to wrap our minds around this.)*

(S)HE'S JUST NASTY AND MEAN.

TRANSFORMED: *(S)he's likely still in pain and possibly feeling insecure, so I can take a deep breath and listen until the nastiness subsides. (S)he just needs to feel heard in order to move forward.*

(S)HE'S SO DISORGANIZED! THE KIDS ALWAYS COME BACK FROM THEIR VISITS MISSING HALF THEIR CLOTHES.

TRANSFORMED: *From now on, I'll be mindful of what I send over so I'm not missing anything when it doesn't come back right away.*

Elena's Meditation for Clarity

Learning to respond rather than react is the cornerstone of your clarity, and your clarity will yield results in your relations with your ex and your family overall. Your aim here is to take the time to practice responsiveness within the quiet of your own being, so you can bring it into your family and divorce process in an effective, efficient way.

Why is clarity important? Because it's in your best interest to get things sorted, recalibrated, and moving forward. When you're clear in your priorities, you can communicate your needs with ease. Thus your family, your soon-to-be ex, and your mediator and/or attorney can also be clear on what matters most to you. When you make your wishes known gracefully, create the outcome you desire, and make the best of what's happening today.

How can you practice this responsiveness within the quiet of your own being? Have a seat, wherever you are. Take five deep breaths; no need for your breathing to be loud, just full, in order to catch a glimpse of your inner ecology today. Settle yourself where you are, knowing you're exactly where you need to be to learn what you'll need to move forward. Grow your spine tall. Continue breathing. Begin to notice the space between your exhalation and your inhalation.

Notice where your mind travels: this thought, that thought. Notice each thought, one at a time; release each thought, one at a time. See each concept that your mind brings up, and let the next breath gently usher it away, like a wave coming ashore to wash the shells and imprints back out to sea. Notice what's left when the exhalation washes the thought away; can you sense the bright moment when your mind is clear and empty?

Remain here for three minutes, perhaps five. Notice how clearheaded you feel when you've finished breathing and observing for that short time. Keep bringing your attention back to the space between the exhalation and the inhalation. In that space, there is freedom. In that space, where no thought exists, is your clarity.

The more you're able to locate this clarity within your own being, increasing your ability to remain quiet inside as challenges arise, the greater the chance you'll be able to manage the more difficult moments of any day in your life.

CHAPTER 5

Peace

Finding Calm Within the Chaos

> When we really delve into the reasons for why we can't let something go, there are only two: an attachment to the past or a fear of the future.
>
> —MARIE KONDO, AUTHOR OF *THE LIFE-CHANGING MAGIC OF TIDYING UP*

For most humans, separation or divorce stirs up a steady stream of doubts, fears, insufficiencies, even rage. Days, months, even years of unspoken worries and concerns begin surfacing, and the turmoil can seem insurmountable at first. This is a chapter devoted to your peace, internally and externally, in your heart, your family, and your future.

How do you define peace? Restfulness. Quiet. Tranquility. Harmony. Accord. Neutrality. These are all states you've experienced previously as qualities or feelings, particularly on holiday, with loving friends or relations, or in calm moments when all is running smoothly.

For Elena, neutrality is the most apt description of peace, and it's been an aim for her in her process of divorcing and creating a sense of true family with her son's father.

Neutrality is a state of holding no tension in your body. It's not weakness or a lack of opinion; in fact, it's a clear strength. It's a state of being in which no external force can move you internally, and you're able to maintain your focus on your aim, no matter what is coming at you. It's an un-shakable internal equilibrium. It took me months to realize that I could cultivate this within myself, and it took years for my son's dad to trust in my steadiness again.

When I realized that what seemed like the most embar-rassing "failure" of my life could actually be transmuted into a greater trust—both in myself and in my relationship as it transformed into friendship—this was the pivot point for me. Indeed, I could create within myself whatever state of being I chose, but it would take my family some time to catch up. I had to be clear, strong, and neutral, even when the people around me were still treating me like the reactive person I'd been in months prior.

So what does neutral feel like? It's not up, it's not down, it's right in the middle. It's not left, it's not right, it's somewhere in the center. It's a place within yourself, and it depends on who you've been.

If you're the one who's never really stood up for yourself, your neutral state might be an easeful but clear stance on what you want and need—and how you'll gladly work or wait peacefully for it. If you're like me, you've been over-reactive and incendiary, so your neutrality is a place of calm listening, actively aware of what's needed for everyone around you to feel safe with you now that you're awake and aware of the aim for all of you—being better apart.

Remember, your current circumstances are not reflective of your future. As with patience, respect, and clarity, feelings that might be interfering with your internal sensation of peace will shift with time and practice. Marie Kondo's concept about decluttering and organizing really speaks to me. Her theory offers a profound truth that applies to both your material possessions and your emotional ties: keep only that which sparks joy, and you will transform your life. I have applied her approach to my own life and have found that making physical space in my environment paves a path to peace for me. Similarly, releasing mental attachments to the past and letting go of concerns about the future are equally transformative practices, essential to creating peace in the present. What does that mean?

Releasing attachments, thoughts, ideas, or habits that no longer serve you is a practice of ridding yourself of opinions and assumptions you've had about how things are and what they're becoming. It's the practice of making space for a new way of thinking and being. Decluttering the swirl of thoughts in your mind helps you remember that this is just a passing moment in time. As the ancient Chinese philosopher and writer Lao Tzu said, "If you are depressed, you are living in the past. If you are anxious, you are living in the future. If you are at peace, you are living in the present." This work is about creating your own internal peace, which will positively impact those around you and alter the energy that follows you through the day. This is why you're here.

Mantras for Peace

Your words and thoughts have profound power on your psyche. Integrating a mantra for peace into your daily routine will help you transcend difficult moments—whether within yourself or with another. The affirmations below are examples that may help you welcome more peace into your life. Recite one silently to yourself or aloud, in the morning after you wake up and before going to bed at night. If you wish, create your own mantra. Be sure it is positive, present, and specific. Repeat the affirmation as often as possible, every day for at least a week in your rotation of affirmations for each element.

I am calm and at peace.

I respond with kindness.

I find peace within myself.

Noticing and releasing my anger opens space for peace in my heart.

Release Your Anger

Anger is not power—it's weakness. Expressions of anger drain your energy, detract from the possibilities for peace, and weaken your reserves. While holding on to anger can be compelling and might even seem morally or ethically important, anger is antithetical to peace. Dig a little deeper and you will realize that anger is actually a deep sadness masked by angry expressions, a sadness that's devolved into destructive thoughts and words. Anger limits the potential for true peace in your life. Especially after many years of frustration, living with anger may be an ingrained habit. However, with small shifts in thought and action, you can transcend and release the negative swirl.

Inspired by peaceful luminary Thich Nhat Hanh's book *Anger,* to mitigate and transform her anger, Elena has found great comfort and real results in studying his work.

"Anger is in us in the form of a seed," according to Thich Nhat Hanh. "The seeds of love and compassion are also there. In our consciousness there are many negative seeds and also many positive seeds. The practice is to avoid watering the negative seeds, and to identify and water the positive seeds every day" (p. 75).

"Holding on to anger is like drinking poison and expecting the other person to die." This quote of disputed origin reminds you to keep your own space clear, because your anger isn't going to affect your ex's process—only yours. Your anger effectively degrades your nervous system, compromises your immune function, and keeps you in a state of emergency that also prevents you from being present for yourself, your kids, your lover, and your bright future. How?

When your body holds on to anger, there is a consistent internal release of a chemical cocktail in the form of hormones. One of those hormones, adrenaline, increases your heart rate and blood pressure, which can compromise your capacity to rebound emotionally. Another hormone, cortisol, known as the stress hormone, can suppress your immune system, which can lead to increased susceptibility to a host of chronic and acute diseases. And when the stress response is sustained over time, it can disrupt the normal homeostasis of the body, which can result in everything from heart disease to digestive problems, memory impairment to sleep disorders, autoimmune disorders to depression.

In the context of divorce, learning to notice, release, and replace your anger is to re-create habits of thinking, feeling, and being, and will ensure that your family has a better chance at a peaceful future.

Movements for Peace

To create stillness in your body, I suggest simple alternating movements that are easy to accomplish no matter where you are in order to drop into a peaceful internal space. Take twenty minutes to walk briskly uphill, on stairs, or at a steep incline on a treadmill. During that time, place your hand on your abdomen and take a few breaths at a time, feeling the breath coming into your belly and then exhaling it out as your navel returns to your spine.

Follow that with a long forward bend, feet hip-width apart on the floor, knees slightly bent, fingertips or hands either on the floor or on your shins (your flexibility will improve over time), focusing on your breathing, your belly moving in and out, opening and returning. Notice the stillness, the sensation of peace there; stay attentive to the breath in your belly. Hold this pose for five to ten breaths, then roll up to stand.

Writing Your Peace

Writing about your circumstances from a positive viewpoint efficiently shifts your thoughts and elevates you to your new reality. If you note the positive points as aspects for which you're grateful, this creates a new story of your future—releasing the past so you can live in the present. Writing down what's working in the form of things you are thankful for—even tiny details—shifts your perspective on even the most painful aspects of your separation.

For example, here is a short list of simple, daily aspects of her life:

My son's face when he's sleeping
My practice space

My kitchen
My dear friends
My morning meditation
Music

Small things help us focus on what's working, what's good, what's bringing us peace, even during turmoil. Each night before you go to sleep (or whatever time works best for you), take out your journal and write what's making you feel thankful, grateful, and peaceful. Write about specific activities that uplift you. This list can become a go-to tool during particularly unsettled moments. My clients find this incredibly helpful when moving from anger to gratitude, inspiring them to move forward. Researchers at Michigan State University's Clinical Psychophysiology Lab have shown that there are neural benefits to expressive writing.

If you're feeling confident enough to take this a step further, I love and practice the technique of replacing a negative experience with a positive one. This manageable, practical habit will shift your perceptions and help you rearrange your inner state. Remember, writing helps move negativity out and usher in positivity.

Elena explains this method of releasing what isn't working in order to replace it with something better. Note any thoughts or facts that still swirl around in your head uncontrollably when you contemplate your separation, breakup, divorce, or any current drama. Start anywhere, and write for two to five minutes each day until you feel like you've noted all the flavors of your current context. Be specific, so you can see it all on paper. Know that this is a process of learning how your mind works and releasing worries, which helps you be more productive, present, and peaceful.

First, your Negative Free Writing exercise will help you offload the most pressing and damaging negative thoughts and associations. Here's an example.

Negative Free Writing

I cannot even see straight. I came in to our weekly meeting calm, kind, and prepared, and she launched into this complete lie and raged about my incapacities as a husband. I couldn't keep my cool, I couldn't keep quiet, and I raged right back.

Next, make a list of the negatives, so you can see each one as an individual thought.

List of Repetitive Negatives

1. (S)he's a liar

2. (S)he's a rager.

3. (S)he causes me to lose my cool every single time.

Next, make a list of the things for which you are grateful. This is where you'll stretch your mind, your heart, and your capacity to significantly shift the landscape of your process. If it's difficult to identify grand positives, start small.

GRATITUDES LIST

1. She's punctual.

2. She's a good mother.

3. She keeps her house organized.

4. She keeps the kids together.

5. She rages only at me; she doesn't say bad things about me to the kids.

_____

_____

I had a client, Isabelle, whose ex-husband's new wife, Chloe, was showing up at the child's parent-teacher meetings. Isabelle focused on how inappropriate and upsetting this was to her. This seeming intrusion led Isabelle to feel threatened. Isabelle wanted me to file a court order stating that the parent-teacher conferences were only for her child's actual legal parents. When we looked into the matter, it became clear that Chloe's intentions were benign, even benevolent—to help with homework and practical matters. As we explored further, Isabelle began to recognize that her child's stepmother was often present at homework time with her child, doing her best during the after-school hours. It became understandable, from all sides.

And while it was difficult for Isabelle to share the "mother" role, the more we looked at what was happening from a broader perspective, the clearer it became that Chloe was actually interested and trying to be helpful. At my urging, Isabelle made lists of her gratitudes, the positive aspects of Chloe's input. Over time, these became the primary points that Isabelle held in her mind. By shifting how she viewed what was happening, she was able to become more accepting, creating greater opportunity for peace.

Releasing Clutter Makes Peace Possible—Next Steps

WRITE A LETTER OF GRATITUDE TO YOUR SPOUSE. This letter is for you; you're not necessarily sending it. It's a way to help you collect your thoughts and refocus your attention on what you've learned and how you've grown as a result of this relationship, both its flourishing and its ending. By writing down the positives and the gratitudes, you open space for yourself to possibly recognize essential lessons, and to evolve and move forward in peace.

FIND YOUR INDEPENDENCE. Many of us struggle when we separate because we've spent the time of our relationship disengaged from some tasks such as bill paying, keeping house, playing with the kids, or maintaining schedules for the family. Some of us have been tending to all of these activities but now find ourselves feeling lost or lonely during unwanted stretches of time without children or responsibility. If this feels familiar and you don't know where to begin, make a plan and write it down. Take one matter at a time. If you are finding yourself with new, unwelcome free time, brainstorm all the things you'd like to do. Recognize the possibilities that this newfound space provides. If you're just familiarizing yourself with your finances, schedule one meeting per week to begin learning, managing, and arranging things. If you've just begun spending quality time with your kids, start by asking them what they love, and keep a sweet journal of your kids' likes and dislikes so they feel your attention. Taking your life into your own hands, one small facet at a time, is how you begin taking huge strides toward your independence, your freedom, your personal deep reconnection with yourself starting in this moment.

VISUALIZE YOURSELF AS A PEACEMAKER. Consider how you want to behave in your world today, and how you want to look back on your separation or divorce. You have two choices: play into drama or chose a path to catalyze peace for your family. You're not lying to yourself if you choose to look at things through the lens of gratitude; instead, you're teaching your friends and family to see things as a visionary—more positively, with more kindness.

Wiring Peace Within Yourself and Your Family

Here are some examples of families who've made peace a priority. Read the short stories and see if you sense any familiarity. Then you'll write a bit more to work toward your family's future peace.

Peaceful Divorce with Children: My Parents

Early in the process of divorcing, my parents argued a fair amount, and those early fights were definitely upsetting to me. At the time, it seemed as though they fought too much, and it made me mad that I had to listen to them complain about each other. In retrospect, I realize that my parents navigated their divorce fairly well.

Over time, they did learn to communicate more clearly by taking turns, which helped them create space for a relatively peaceful divorce for us. They spoke almost daily and were careful to maintain similar rules in both households. They cohosted birthday parties and graduations for my brother and me, and although early on there were difficult times, they spoke with each other reasonably well.

When they first separated, I asked my mother why they were divorcing. She told me that they had grown-up problems that I didn't have to worry about, and that I should just enjoy being a kid. Both my parents sat me down and told me that even though they were getting divorced, they were still my parents, and they were both still in charge. While we had plenty of bumps in the road as a family, they understood the importance of peace between themselves and in our family, and we children were their first priority. Today my parents are, in a particular way, dear friends.

Peaceful Divorce Without Children: Sam and Jesse

Five years after getting married at age twenty-four, Jesse announced that their marriage was based more on friendship than it was on romantic love, and both deserved more. Sam was shocked and crushed, but didn't want to feel like the last six years had been a total waste. After two months of teary days and nights, Sam came to realize that despite his initial distress, separating was the right choice—it was the beginning of the next stage of life. Both partners expressed a desire to exit their relationship from a place of peace. Each person wished the other well in moving forward. The benefits? They were able to remember and recognize the qualities that had drawn them together, which helped them rewire their future relationship and co-manage their jointly owned property for years.

Theirs is an example of clear aim, peaceful communication, and willingness to let a strong friendship remain intact.

Peaceful Parting with Only One Peaceful Participant

José and Eloise had two children and owned two homes. Eloise was a physician; José, an artist. Formerly the primary financial support in the household, Eloise learned that José had been having an affair for the final two years of their marriage. Though devastated, Eloise wanted to try counseling. Emotionally, José had already moved on and was unwilling to continue with the marriage. He also expected to receive alimony as well as child support, and wished to share custody of the kids.

Eloise became enraged and was the first to file for divorce. Although he was legally entitled to a significant amount of money from her, he chose to receive only what he needed and did not become defensive when she blamed all their problems on him. He remained calm, factual, and peaceful. He took time to write her a letter of apology, owning up to his part in their breakup. Initially she refused to sit down and make any attempt at an agreement, and vowed that she would never speak to him again. José understood that she was hurt and consistently treated her with compassion and generosity. Over time, while still angry and not interested in a friendship with José, Eloise grew willing to sit down and arrive at a reasonable resolution. José's patience and willingness to establish peace was crucial for this positive outcome.

Your Peaceful Parting: Listening and Listing

As a couple, you may be as lucky as the pairs in the first two stories—both committed to upholding ease with an organized and peaceful approach. If you're coupled with a partner who seems unwilling to create peace, maintain your commitment to clear communication and your own personal peace. Validate your former partner's side by listening, then repeating it back, asking if you missed anything. Do this calmly and without judgment. Make space for your ex to truly feel heard. Ideally, when you each express how you feel, you will name your own emotion rather than criticizing or blaming each other. This is a skill that takes work. If your ex communicates blame, instead of criticizing back, do your best to reflect the underlying emotion.

For instance, if he/she says, "You are always such an inconsiderate jerk. I am standing here waiting for you and I have somewhere else to be," you can respond with, "I am hearing you say you feel angry and frustrated that I am late." Then, ask if there is more. Do not react. Simply reflect what you are hearing and allow the download for several minutes. Be punctual next time. Creating space for your former partner to feel heard may pave the way for productive communication going forward.

The need for validation is tremendous and can be an incredible salve. Over time, your example will help everyone in your family. If you find yourself frustrated because you are doing everything in your power to be peaceful, yet your spouse continues to complicate things, you may need to take a step back and reassess the situation. It is not always possible to engage in face-to-face communication or to even actively engage. With a particularly difficult dynamic, you may need to request that communication be via email and be limited to essential matters. You may even set up a separate email so that you are not caught off-guard and can control when you wish to read it. For some, making and referring to an ongoing list with the goal of transforming how you feel around your ex may help you to begin to press reset.

Quick exercise: Make two columns. In the left column, write down the uncontrollably difficult emotions. *Enraged* is a good example. In the right column, directly opposite the first word, write in the opposite emotion: in this case, *serene* seems perfect. Then say aloud or to yourself the rewired emotion: "I am serene." Then repeat this affirmation or mantra quietly or silently to yourself the next time you're enraged.

Visualizing Peace Opens Space for New Possibilities

Visualize. Internalize. Realize. The first step is the most crucial. However, once you begin visualizing your peace, hopefully you'll find that you'll feel more settled almost instantly. Note the people, places, situations, and occasions that bring you peace. Take your time and write them all down. There is always a common denominator among them. Name the commonality so it enters your awareness. Keep this list close to you, adding to it as images come to mind. Use this list to practice creating and cultivating peace when challenging moments in your divorce process enter your space. As you visualize your clear thoughts of peace with specificity, you will surprise yourself with your ability to remove yourself from feelings of chaos and unrest.

When Elena's separation process first began:

I was so blinded by fear and anger that peace was the furthest thing from my mind. When I met my coach, Lauren, her homework had me writing a lot. I began to see what I'd done to hold myself back, and what I could do going forward to invite peace into my situation in small ways. That was the beginning of my family's opening. As I've remembered to host peace within myself in the tougher moments, my behavior has shifted and my son's dad has begun to trust me. Although it took about two years to come to fruition, that was the beginning of our friendship. Remember to cultivate your own internal peace throughout your process, and everyone around you will benefit.

Stopping the Gossip

At many points during the aftermath of your initial separation, you'll find people around you interested in gossip, negativity, and vengeful conversation. Remember that gossip degrades us, both physically and emotionally, and while it may feel good in the moment, it actually amplifies anguish and creates a long-lasting anger that is difficult to erase. If you need to vent about your ex to your trusted circle, do your best to remain kind in your words. When you are feeling angry, do your best to consider all sides. Think long-term. While it may feel good in this moment, you and your children will not benefit from negativity. Keep gossip out of your conversations to truly commit to peace.

The extended family on my mom's side spend one week together every summer at a reunion. Because all the grandchildren and children are there, my father often pops in and out throughout the week. He'll get the kids ice cream and take them horseback riding. Though my mom has been at peace with my dad regarding her issues with him, her brother (my uncle) remained angry. Throughout the week he'd make unkind comments about my father, reminding us all of unpleasant days far in the past. While my uncle may have felt that he was supporting his sister, he was mired in forty-year-old gossip and anger. Remember that when you speak negatively of your ex to people who care about you, you're building a wall of negativity that others may not forget. Even if you have moved past your anger, they may not. At the writing of this book, I had that long-overdue conversation with my uncle. He expressed surprise and really worked at releasing any remaining negative energy. This past summer, our gathering was much more pleasant and peaceful.

No matter who's speaking, when disparaging things are said about your ex, your child will feel it as a deep, internal conflict. You two parents created this child, and it diminishes that child to hear gossip and negativity shared, even if it happens to be true. Move your family in the direction of peace by taking care with your words and encouraging those with whom you're surrounded to do the same. Even if your ex is a monster, just focus on the future and the healing of your family.

While it's important to express your feelings, recognize the distinction between talking about your feelings and gossiping. Choose wisely when sharing your personal stories. Bestselling author and professor Brené Brown has extensively researched and written about what she has called the power of vulnerability. She asserts while there is great value in allowing yourself to be vulnerable, be careful about the people with whom you share.

If you have someone in your life who always fans the flames of gossip, courageously let that person know you are choosing the high road, and/or you wish move forward toward friendship, or at least amicability, in the future. If you have children, Elena and I encourage you wholeheartedly to write this out, then state your truth out loud.

I honor my child's parent. I am committed to using my voice to uplift this situation, and honor my child and my family with my words and my actions. I am here to uphold peace for myself, my child, and my family.

As always, if our exact words do not feel comfortable, please tailor this statement to suit you using language that is most natural.

Breathing and Meditation for Peace

If you have children, you know that the most peaceful, connected times can be created in the minutes prior to bedtime, when all is quiet, and you're able to forge a conscious connection between you. In those times, both with your kids and with yourself, breathing peacefully can mean the difference between fitful sleep and deeply restful slumber.

Meditation for Peace to Begin and End Your Day

Peace within you creates a safe space within your home; peace opens possibility and potency for all. Elena has created a meditation based on her experience that will help you wake up and end your day with a feeling of peace in your body, your mind, and your heart.

Upon awakening in the morning, brush your teeth, leave your devices off, and sit up in your bed up against the wall or headboard, or on a chair, or on a cushion on the floor. Make sure you're sitting in a comfortable position. If it's best to have your legs straight, do what's easiest. As you settle into a few minutes of observation, begin to notice the cadence of your breathing. For so many separating couples, the drama and difficulty makes it hard to stay connected to yourself, to your body, to your health. This daily moment to yourself will help you bring your body back to a healthy internal rhythm and will help bring to the fore your neutral, clear vision for the future.

First, spend a minute or two noticing where you breathe. Is it in your chest, or can you breathe a bit more deeply, into your belly? As you watch, you'll notice your breathing can get a bit deeper, more nourishing. Stay with that for about ten breaths. Observe the length of your thoughts, the sensation of space between one thought and the next. Notice that as your breathing deepens, you might feel a bit more spacious in your mind.

Then begin to let your breathing be natural and see if anything else shifts. Let a few minutes pass, just feeling your body, making space, listening, breathing.

As you continue breathing, consider your next step post-separation. If you're moving, see your absolute dream home in your mind. The gorgeous bedroom, the light streaming in, your kitchen, your ideal living space. Be creative, be free, be imaginative, be fearless. Design it. If you're staying put, do the same visualizing, just in your current space. What can be released now? What will stay? What will be reworked? Let a full, clear, detailed image arise in your mind about your peaceful, peace-filled sanctuary to come. Even if you're staying where you are and these changes cannot be made at this time, consider releasing some old belongings or making one small shelf your prayer space, where you can go for figurative shelter to retreat within yourself.

At the end of each day, sit in the same space and begin your observations as before. Instead of envisioning the future, though, prior to sleep, notice one by one any doubt, fear, or insecurity cropping up in your mental space, and become aware of how that thought affects your breathing capacity. As you sit, allow each breath to deepen, and with each exhalation, allow each thought to dissipate and be released.

Once you feel more space inside, allow your breathing to return to its normal cadence and sit quietly until you feel more peaceful and steady.

Legal Wisdom

In his book *Anger,* a practical guidebook to navigating our emotional landscape, meditation teacher Thich Nhat Hanh asks us to communicate about our experience of anger in a simple, truthful fashion. He recommends that we say it as it is.

> In the past, we were allied in making each other suffer more, allied in the escalation of anger. . . . Both of us were victims of our anger. We made a hell for each other. Now I want to change. I want us to become allies, so we can protect each other . . . and transform our anger together. Let us build a better life from now on. . . . I need your help. I need your support. I need your collaboration. I cannot succeed without you. (p. 49)

Asking earnestly for collaboration opens direct possibilities for teamwork. You're straightforwardly offering your support and asking for reciprocity. It is easiest to practice this simple request and commitment on your part with your kids and your friends, and it might even work with your ex. Try it with your kids first, because their willingness to play fair and collaborate is likely more present than what we might find in most adults. Developing this collaborative spirit, according to Thich Nhat Hanh, is awakening.

Before you meet with your attorney, do what you can to clear out your own anger and negativity. Eliminating such emotional clutter opens space for you to carefully, creatively design your peaceful future. Just by writing down a few of your most destructive, angry thoughts, you can begin to create some distance between you and that negativity.

Studies done by researchers at Eastern Michigan University demonstrate that personal writing helps to relieve stress and anxiety. It's even been found that mood and immune function was enhanced in college students who were asked to write about their most traumatic experiences for fifteen to twenty minutes per day for four days.

Bear in mind that your lawyer may not agree with your pledge for a peaceful stance. Far from a weakness or a liability, your commitment to peace is both your power and your practice.

How will you maintain your personal peace when there's ample opportunity to generate drama? Give yourself permission to feel tranquil internally, so that your participation in external matters is laced with peace. I've often counseled clients to give a little, to offer an unexpected overture that the other party would never anticipate. Typically that will ease the conflict as well as the path forward. Particularly in a heated legal context, it's crucial to cultivate a habit of peacefulness. Act the way you wish to think, and your mindset will actually shift.

Unprocessed raw emotion is a drain on your body and your future happiness. When you learn to recognize and manage your anger so you can respond rather than react, your choices and requests concerning money, home, and children will be more measured and helpful to all parties. If this makes you uncomfortable or feels unreasonable, remember that acknowledging, accepting, and navigating deep emotional states takes practice. With slow, measured effort, you can separate your emotions from the facts and be a force for peace in your family.

Practical Tips for Peace

CHOOSE YOUR BATTLES. Listen to what your attorney advises, and, at the same time, listen to your instincts. Sometimes walking away is the only path for peace

TAKE A WALK, WRITE, OR TAKE TEN DEEP BREATHS. Make sure you do this prior to emailing your attorney—in fact, prior to any interaction. Remember that each contact has a cost, so be practical and save your chits for the important matters.

BE READY TO BE FLEXIBLE. If your ex is refusing mediation, have your lawyer suggest it to the other lawyer, and be ready to change your response to what's not in the sphere of your control.

FIGURE OUT WHAT IS MOST IMPORTANT FOR YOUR EX AND SEE HOW YOU MAY GRANT IT. Once we dig in, I've observed that the two sides often care about differing possessions or issues, and it can be easier than we think.

MODEL PEACE. Offer an extended hand or a pleasant smile or exchange a kindness without expectation of reciprocation. You are becoming an example of peace.

CONSIDER LETTING SOMETHING GO. If you can afford to move forward materially or emotionally with taking less or giving more in your divorce resolution, consider letting something go. Often in the moment we hold on to feelings or desire for possessions that in retrospect hold little consequence or importance to us. Releasing attachment paves the path to peace.

RECOGNIZE THAT PEACE IS A CHOICE AND TAKES EFFORT. Adjust your expectations so that peace has time to become habit. It takes two people to argue, but only one person to start a process of peace.

Peace for Your Children

In your children's eyes, you are still a family. Help them have a peaceful, steady childhood with these few practices.

MAINTAIN PEACE AND SIMILAR RULES BETWEEN YOUR HOUSE-HOLDS. Whenever possible, do your best to keep your parenting aligned, and refrain from speaking negatively about your child's other parent. This will help your children feel stable, cared for, and secure. We all know that for many children, transitions between homes can be challenging, but far more damaging is inconsistency and discord between the separating parents.

EMPHASIZE TEAMWORK AND CLEAR BOUNDARIES FOR ALL. Elena held family meetings to keep the lines of communication open, which helped her son's dad, their sitter, and their son feel safe and in a routine. Our sense of belonging in this world begins in the context of family, and a sense of security in our homes yields creativity and clarity as we get older. While I was growing up, my parents had family meetings several times a year, involving my two parents, sometimes their significant others, and me. This gave everyone a time and a safe space to openly discuss the boundaries and rules in both households, which helped me feel connected and respected in both places. And while I found these meetings incredibly irritating as a teenager, in retrospect I recognize the gift of peace those meetings provided.

GIVE MORE THAN YOU THINK YOU CAN OR SHOULD. When considering how to make requests that might be met with resistance, consider what you're willing to give in exchange—even concessions that might be well past your comfort zone. For example, perhaps you wish to move to another state with your child. When you present that request, offer more holidays and perhaps extended vacations (even summers) with the other parent, in order to help level the playing field for all. Perhaps you can agree to allow the child to be raised in the other parent's faith. Consider what he or she cares about, and offer that in exchange for a difficult ask of your own. In a dear friend's case, she gave more than seemed intelligent early on, opting to lower the amount of child support and diverting that money into her daughter's college fund.

Another example—I had a client whose ex insisted that their son attend school in his town rather than in hers. She had a clear case that she could've advanced to have her child's friends and activities nearer to her. Instead, she chose long-term peace and let their son attend school near his father. By the time he began high school, he'd chosen to attend a school closer to his mother. They avoided an unnecessary, unforgettable battle, and in this case, taking the long view was key to upholding priceless peace for her family.

Last, you may have to advise your attorney that you are navigating your divorce with the long-term goal of peace. Even with peace as a goal skillful counsel can still advocate from a place of strength. If your attorney cannot do that, it might be time to shift gears to find someone who does. Please note some lawyers love the adversarial process and are stuck in the idea of zealous representation. They may fail to consider that their approach may cause significant collateral damage that will long impact you and your family.

Highlight this: This is not about the win. This is about your family's experience of tranquility as you all move forward. It's important for all of you.

Peace for Yourself

Starting today, your magic word is SELF-CARE. Especially on the days when you know you'll be having difficult conversations or feared interactions with your ex or attorneys, one act of generosity for yourself, advancing your own joy every single day, is nonnegotiable. Peace can flow naturally only when you feel nourished and fulfilled, and when you take care of yourself, you have more capacity to take care of everyone else.

Self-Care Ideas

Give yourself "me time" to do nothing at all.

Take a walk.

Go for a drive.

Book a healing treatment.

Read a book.

Take a nap.

Sit for a short meditation or breathe ten attentive breaths.

Call a friend. Express sadness when you need compassionate support, but limit complaints. Actively try to shift your conversation to a positive note. Surround yourself with people who offer loving, supportive counsel.

Listen to an uplifting or edifying podcast.

Write for three minutes in your journal. Be sure to balance each negative sentence or message with several positives to counterbalance. Remember, words have power.

CHAPTER 6

Forgiveness

Letting Go and Moving Forward

> You must forgive those who hurt you, even if what they did is unforgivable in your mind. You will forgive them not because they deserve to be forgiven, but because you don't want to suffer and hurt yourself every time you remember what they did to you.
>
> —DON MIGUEL RUIZ, *THE MASTERY OF LOVE*

Forgiveness is messy and complicated. It's a cleansing and a release, an ending and a beginning. It's the letting go of blame; it's the invitation offered by grace. It's not easy, but when it's done, we realize it's not hard either. Forgiveness is the gift you give to yourself. Then it makes its way to touch everyone else in your world.

To define forgiveness, I find it useful to think about the concept of neutrality. Neutral in this case can be defined as a lack of tension in your physical body, your emotional state, or your mind. When I'm neutral, I'm free of reactivity, I'm clear, I'm peaceful, and I'm forgiving of the most important person—myself. This is a daily practice for me, and I encourage you to join me in the most liberating game around. Forgive yourself! Do it again and again, today, tomorrow. I'm not saying you *must* forgive your ex. I'm suggesting that right now, in this moment, you practice this: forgive *yourself* for the choices you've made, and set yourself free. Rather than continuously looping the idea that your relationship was a mistake, choose to forgive yourself so you have the chance to grow, learn, and change. Allow yourself the option of a clean slate, a newness you've never known, with all the knowledge you've accrued, a fresh start.

If you're feeling resistant to this concept of forgiveness, know this: forgiveness is a form of self-nourishment, self-nurturing, and even self-love. The forgiveness I'm describing here is precursor to understanding true compassion, which is essentially a state of forgiveness that you can give your children and carry into your next relationship. In modeling forgiveness and its by-product, compassion, you ameliorate the environment within your family and have a hand in creating kindness and understanding going forward.

Practically speaking, forgiveness can take shape in a few ways. You might let go of the idea of a different or better past. You might come to understand that the hurtful words and actions of others come from their own pain, emotional incapacity, or ignorance. With forgiveness, you might find yourself capable of accepting what is rather than what could have been. And you might build your future from there, with positivity, elegance, and grace.

When you are filled with uncontrollable emotions, just as we discussed in the context of clarity, the emotional brain co-opts the thinking brain, and you're easily swept into the negative swirl that separation and divorce can become. And while you cannot control everything that happens, by practicing the neutral mind of forgiveness, you'll experience emotional stability, and you'll be far more likely to respond rather than react. Instead of holding yourself hostage by holding a grudge, you're freeing yourself and everyone around you by making space for forgiveness in any of the forms mentioned in the previous paragraph.

Forgiveness can be elusive. If you feel ashamed, infuriated, vulnerable, or sad, it's because you're in the midst of a personal human earthquake. Regardless of who initiated it—you, your ex, or both of you—the ground on which you stand is unsteady and unstable. Forgiveness will give you the stable foundation from which to build new ways of relating, a visionary vantage point, and a new start. With forgiveness as your anchor and true compassion as your compass, you'll be able to provide yourself with the sturdy support necessary to move forward beyond your separation and divorce.

Mantra for Forgiveness

I'm Sorry. Please Forgive Me. Thank You. I Love You.

When there is an obstacle—be it an attitude, an action, or a circumstance—from this point on you can consider the freedom that forgiveness will invite into your life. It begins with a full breath in, right here, right now. As you inhale, you're taking in the oxygen and the spaciousness that comes with even the slightest hint of forgiveness for yourself or the other—especially when it seems insurmountable. Now you're ready to enlist a set of statements known as the Ho'Oponopono Prayer. These four phrases render true forgiveness accessible and relatable.

This practice focuses on healing both yourself and the other, in the quiet of your own mind and body. It ensures that you're relating to the highest in yourself and the other, rather than the lowest. In repeating it, you're creating more space for more peace. The practice is four simple statements, involving repentance, forgiveness, gratitude, and love.

And you needn't say it aloud; you may say it to yourself and notice how it changes your inner state.

I'M SORRY. I'm sorry for my part; I'm sorry for not addressing this sooner. You're apologizing to yourself and others in a kind and true way for your role in the matter.

PLEASE FORGIVE ME. Forgive me for the confusion and suffering that I've added, whether I've played a small part, let things happen, or committed acts that have hurt others.

THANK YOU. This note of gratitude is for all of it. For the discord, the strife, the drama, the pain, all of which has led to this burgeoning understanding. Thank yourself, your ex, the Universe.

I LOVE YOU. Say it to yourself, your body, your soul, even your ex, everyone. It was once true. This is the most powerful aspect—it's helping you rewire your mind to open.

Movement and Posture for Forgiveness

Place your left hand on your heart space, at the center of your chest. Place your right hand on top of your left hand. Take a moment to simply feel how your body responds. You might begin to feel more relaxed, more steady. Take one or two breaths there.

Now place your attention on your thoughts. With your hands in this position, notice if your thoughts come more slowly, more quietly, more spaciously. Give a couple of breaths to this observation, just watching and noticing. By now you will likely have a greater sense of command over your mind, your thoughts, and your body. This will help you find your way back to a feeling of understanding. It will give you access to your creativity so you can find solutions to what's currently in need of solving.

Gently inhale and open your arms out to the sides, as though embracing the globe, the earth. Exhale and return your hands to your heart. Repeat that movement about five times, consciously emanating through your hands and heart the resonance and feeling of forgiveness. This simple practice begins to shift your interior state to a more open, expansive, permissive space.

Pause for a minute and reflect on how you feel right now.

Facing the "You" Factor

Whereas anger is an outward burst of emotion caused by something you perceive to be unjust, shame faces inward. It's insidious—even *you* may not notice it.

No matter the circumstances, divorce can be a breeding ground for shame—for the parents and even for the children. When I was a kid, the married parents of my friends would often talk about how great I was doing, despite my circumstances. They considered this a compliment, but it never felt that positive. It felt diminishing, as though I was broken, my family was broken, my home was broken. When I was in my twenties, a boyfriend who'd grown up in a very close nuclear family would often note that his childhood was *different* from mine. I always thought that word *different* meant his was *better*, and mine was somehow *defective*.

So often, divorce makes a person feel ashamed, damaged, weakened. You're here to transform and reframe your thinking and life so that you don't feel embarrassed because of your separation or divorce. Author, teacher, and scholar Brené Brown has done significant work on shame, pointing us back to embracing vulnerability, revising the story of weakness into one of triumph.

How do we do this? Recognize, apologize, and forgive.

Recognize

You may feel you deserve to suffer because of the circumstances of your divorce. If that is the case, your apology is your triumph. Nobody needs to suffer any further. It's time to acknowledge your role and move forward toward an apology.

Apologize

This is your time to craft an articulate apology to yourself, and to anyone you've hurt, for whatever is haunting you. This can take days or weeks, but begin now. By writing out the matters that haunt you and offering words of apology, you're recasting your shame into connection and creating a new playing field for everyone involved. This will lead you directly into forgiveness, an important skill to cultivate in your life.

Forgive

Especially if you're on the other side of the story and you've been deeply wronged, you have similar work to do. Recognition of yourself is important here too in order to acknowledge that you'd allowed things to occur because you'd had a certain set of tools at that time. And given those tools in that specific setting, you did your best. Your forgiveness in this case is for yourself, acknowledging your role, forgiving yourself for what's happened, for allowing it. Your time to suffer is over as you read this, and moving forward is the most evolutionary, revolutionary act you can commit for your family. Forgiveness begins here.

Writing for Forgiveness

When you find yourself confronted with a difficult situation during your process, sometimes a simple list of pros and cons can be clarifying as you move through situations that may seem unforgivable.

Jane had been divorced from her ex, Robert, for nearly four years. And even though Jane had remarried within that time, Robert was insinuating himself into her life in ways that were uncomfortable for her. He clearly wanted to stay close to her even as she found new love, even finding a way to show up on their vacation in order to drop their son off to her—in Asia! And while they shared custody of the child, Robert clearly did not respect her boundaries at all. Jane was reasonably angry at him for continuing to interfere, and her breaking point came when Robert actually rented a place quite near to where Jane and her new husband rented a summer vacation home. It was all too much for her, and understandably so.

She came to me to discuss filing a legal action to prevent him from doing that. As we carefully explored and discussed the situation, I realized that Robert was anxious and feeling powerless. He was still living alone and hadn't dated since their divorce. She shared that he felt threatened by the thought of his boy being away with Jane and her new husband, in a town where no one knew he even existed. That too is a reasonable sensation for a newly separated parent, and many of my clients have had it. The key is to transform it—but more on that shortly.

Of course Jane still wondered if filing a legal action to modify their agreement would help. So we simply listed the possible positive and negative outcomes; it was that easy.

Pros for filing a modification of their judgment (so Jane and her new man could travel without her ex nearby):

She could enjoy a peaceful summer vacation in her new household.

The child would have a month free of his parents' bickering and disagreements.

Robert would likely think twice before he tried to insinuate himself on their vacation again.

Cons against filing a modification of their judgment:

The bigger picture may be lost on Robert, enabling him to continue to show up on vacations and elsewhere. This might even prevent him from seeking love for himself with a new woman.

She risked being denied the modification by the court, which would mean he would be there for the summer and might even be more self-righteous than ever.

A fair amount of money would be spent on attorneys' fees, and she and Robert would both have to take time off from work to manage those proceedings.

Their son would likely experience the impact of both Robert's anger and her escalating frustration. Negativity would abound.

After looking at the pros and cons carefully, Jane determined that if she sought this modification in court, it wouldn't solve the bigger problem, and it could easily create more problems and animosity. So instead of filing, Jane moved through her anger by making another list. This time she wrote down what she viewed as her ex's weaknesses (insecurity, loneliness, neediness, disorganization, reactivity), and the consequences of them (weak family ties, few community ties, feeling an extreme need to show his son that he is in the picture no matter what).

She did this for a few weeks, adding to her list each day. Here's the gold of this practice: by taking the time to list and map his struggle, she was able to find compassion and release some of her anger toward her ex. She realized that he was not an ill-defined, amorphous monster ready to strike at any minute. He was committing pitiable, small-minded actions to which a strong woman like Jane could choose her reactions. And based on her list, and what she came to understand about him, she chose to respond instead of react. That's evolution.

On the other hand, if her ex had been my client, I'd have had him do the same. List Jane's actions, behaviors, and traits. He would have seen that she was just a woman seeking love, recognition, peace, and quality time with her boy and her new partner. He would have gathered that she doesn't hold ill will toward him—she just needed to move on with her life and turn the page. He'd have been able to begin the slow process of healing his own heart to find his new path—possibly a new partner and love.

Once Jane was clear about her ex's motivations, she was able to reach out to Robert to set up a meeting. And as soon as Robert walked in the room, I could tell that Jane had forgiven him. From years of experience, I have reached the point where I can see where exes are in their forgiveness process. She was able to make authentic, caring conversation, and her countenance and energy remained easeful as she interacted with him.

We then established clear boundaries that made Jane feel safe, and we gave Robert a few days to spend with their kid during her vacation so he didn't feel invisible. She chose days that worked for her, so she and her husband could spend time reconnecting and having some welcome time off while Robert watched their son. By writing her lists, Jane found forgiveness, and that landed her in a state of ongoing, consistent compassion for her ex. Without going to court, we arrived at a productive resolution and set up a positive process for the future.

Jane was further inspired to make lists regarding her own strengths and weaknesses. She began to recognize her predilection for dwelling on what annoyed her, and began consciously tapping into a forward-thinking approach to her work and her parenting. This work was liberating and significantly constructive for her. She began finding compassion for people around her, and the ever-elusive compassion for herself.

Forgiveness and Betrayal

Joyce came into my office before she'd decided to file for divorce. I remember when she came in and said, "Something just doesn't feel right." We spoke about her options, and I explained my preference for a nontoxic approach if she did decide to end her marriage. She left and I didn't hear anything from her for a few months.

One day she called and said she was ready to file. Things with her husband, Darren, had gone from bad to worse. During one conversation, he'd accused her of cheating. A lightbulb went off in Joyce's head. "Are you having an affair?" she asked him. Darren went silent—and that's when Joyce knew. Although he insisted the affair was over and that the woman was no longer working in his office, when Joyce told him the next day she wanted a divorce, Darren seemed relieved. They worked with a mediator and were able to agree on all facets of their agreement. While the finishing touches were being made on their agreement, however, Joyce made a discovery: Darren's affair wasn't over, as he'd said it was.

And it wasn't with a woman at work, as he'd previously indicated.

Darren's affair had been with Joyce's best friend. And she was pregnant.

This was one of the very few times in my work as an attorney that
I experienced anger at a client's ex. Joyce, though, wanted to move
forward with the agreement as it was. Impressively, she'd harnessed
what appeared to be a superhuman source of strength. She shared
with me that, long ago, she'd learned the power of choice. She realized that she couldn't control what others did; she could only control
what *she* did.

Joyce and Darren came to a peaceful agreement of shared custody, temporarily arranging to nest (minus the new girlfriend). To
clarify, in divorce cases, nesting means the children stay in the family home, and the parents come in and out when it's their turn to be
with the kids. As her lawyer, I wanted to be sure it was what she
truly wanted—not something she felt obliged to do out of a misguided sense of generosity.

And in the end, Joyce granted herself the ultimate justice by embracing the opportunity to start fresh with a man who'd disrespected
her so deeply. She continued to support and respect him as the father
of their children, but rather than succumbing to anger or bitterness,
Joyce practiced forgiveness for her ex and his actions, which landed
her in what I deemed to be an extraordinary state of compassion.
Her family still enjoys the benefits of this gift to this day.

Mantra for Forgiving Yourself

(Especially After an Emotional Outburst)

Elena finds self-forgiveness one of the most vital, rejuvenating
forces in the process of a graceful divorce. Especially if you're

reading this and have recently done or said something you regret, forgiving yourself is an important source of comfort, as
well as a good example you set for your family. If you have children, they will need to learn this most of all. And if you're the
child of a messy divorce, this may not feel natural to you. Unless you've done a good deal of emotional work, it's likely that
your default is to blame yourself. This practice begins to change
that.

> During this time, forgive yourself for any actions you've
> taken for which you feel ashamed. Self-forgiveness is an
> extremely elegant practice that puts you on the mend psy-
> chologically, emotionally, and physically. Forgiveness is the
> ultimate salve for most families, and it begins with you.
>
> Say to yourself mentally or aloud: "I forgive and release
> myself from judgment, shame, and blame. Now is when I
> move forward." Repeat this a few times. The repetition of
> this simple sentiment sets you up for a new possibility again
> and again.
>
> These mantras are helpful in redirecting negative thought-
> energy and in remapping your mind. Again, you may re-
> peat them mentally or aloud, choosing one or all, or perhaps
> writing your own.

> *Today I give my eyes to receive beauty, and I trust in the order of*
> *my life.*
> *Today I give up living with my heart closed, and I choose to live*
> *with my heart open.*
> *Today I give up all traces of grudges. I choose to be available to*
> *more and more love.*

Breathing for Forgiveness

Elena has used these simple practices to locate forgiveness in a moment, and shares them often with individuals and couples alike. You don't need to have any yoga or meditation experience to use them, but if you do, you'll appreciate the mechanics of the pause they bring about.

This is the life your soul chose in order to learn what you've come here to learn. Blaming stops here, right now. Why? If you continue to blame, either yourself or anyone else, you'll keep your body and mind in a state of stress, negativity, and pain. To relinquish the idea of what your life should've or could've looked like, welcome a few nourishing breaths into your body. One breath at a time, let the thoughts in your mind slowly become still. Take five to ten breaths right here until your mind slows down. Then continue reading.

Please place your left hand on your heart; then place your right hand on top of it. You may use this hand placement often to quiet your thoughts and soften your behavior. Take a few moments here to sense the cadence of your heart's rhythm. Surrounding your heart is your pericardium, an envelope of sorts that contains your heart perfectly within it. Be sensitive to the quality of the energy there, between that sheath and the muscle of the heart itself. Take the next few breaths to simply loosen any held or tense sensations in that space.

With this hand placement, or mudra, you're sourcing and distributing softness throughout your entire body, from your heart outward. Only you can create the conditions for more ease and stability in your being, right this moment. Spend the next few breaths cultivating that opening.

Recognize that your current reality is one aspect of a much longer path. Realize that your heart is ready for compassion— for yourself, for the other whose immense pain has caused him/her to inflict pain, and for everyone who's been touched by your situation. Know that your forgiveness of yourself and others is a portal to your emotional and mental freedom. Congratulations on taking these moments of forgiveness into your own hands.

Priming Your Mind for Forgiveness

Elena's Forgiveness Story

Once upon a time, I had a habit of chronically blaming everyone else for my misery and misfortune, and had no connection to forgiveness at all. With a few good teachers and moments of clear listening, I realized that forgiveness was the only way for me to craft a better attitude and a better outcome for my family. Forgiveness means I've stopped wishing that things would've gone differently. Forgiveness means that rather than moving forward with my heart closed and dark, I'm moving forward with my heart open and light.

Forgiveness is the commencement of compassion. It comes in healing waves, tidal surges that have helped me face my own as well as others' actions. The first wave arrived the month after my husband and I chose to separate, when I began to recognize that the most revolutionary act I could consider would be to tell the truth, open my heart, and forgive.

I allowed that wave to wash over me, to begin cleansing me of fear and anger and help me move onward, with my heart available and ready for magic.

The second wave of forgiveness came when I met my coach, who pointed out that my own actions had played a significant role in the demise of my marriage, which I hadn't even considered. She taught me to ask for forgiveness and to forgive myself. That self-forgiveness turned out to be the real revolution I'd always sought. It's a practice I follow to this day. Whenever my thoughts are darkening, I ask myself, "What can I forgive in myself right this moment? What can I do to open my heart again and ease this pain—my own or someone else's?"

This current of forgiveness keeps washing through me, day after day, in my work and in my studies. Meditation and yoga cleanse the anger, fear, dread, and sadness from me almost daily, leaving me clear, openhearted, ready. Now my son's dad and I have created a new sensation of family. We communicate compassionately and steadily, and we hold one another up when the situation feels shaky. Forgiveness is real, and it works.

Review, Release, and Recalibrate

Elena offers this daily practice as a way to connect to forgiveness as a simple, daily ritual.

At night, when you're lying down to sleep and are getting quiet, consider if there is anything you're still rolling over in your mind, something you feel you could have done more gracefully or should have handled more thoughtfully. As soon as you've identified that action or attitude in yourself, place your left hand on your heart and say mentally or aloud, "I forgive myself wholeheartedly for this thought/attitude/action." Say it a few times softly to yourself until you feel the weight lift. If appropriate, design and deliver an appropriate and heartfelt apology for causing pain, harm, or heartache to anyone affected by your actions.

Legal Wisdom

Forgiveness gets easier when you're prepared, but here are a few that always surprise my clients.

Surprise 1. You might have to forgive your local laws.

There's one thing no one tells you before you go through a divorce: The law is not always going to feel fair. Some of the laws may seem absurd in your particular situation, and your work is to move forward with the assumption that the laws were written with the best intention for all involved. You will likely need to forgive the legislative and judicial branches of your country and state just as much as you will need to forgive yourself and your ex. In this context, forgiveness means acceptance.

As your divorce proceedings commence, your lawyer will guide you through the local laws, and, at some point, you will most likely be told of a law that seems unfathomable to you. Shocked clients often say something like "This wasn't the case for my friend." Then I probe a bit and learn the friend lives in Ohio (or some other state). Indeed, the laws in New York and Massachusetts, where I practice, may be starkly different from the laws in Ohio and every other state. One client was understandably furious that local law forbade him from paying child support directly to his college-age daughter, obliging him to send it to his ex instead. He viewed this law as a great injustice to both himself and his daughter, and would compulsively mention it every time he spoke to either of them. His frustration was destructive to their family dynamic and kept their relationship in a negative holding pattern. Forgiving the seemingly ridiculous laws that make things difficult is a vital step to accepting what's true and moving on in the best possible way.

Remember too that laws are written in broad terms to create the most universally positive outcomes, even though that isn't always the case. For now, consider the possibility that the law that is currently causing you grief may actually be helping another family or another person's child. Forgive the lawmakers for enacting a law that creates adverse consequences for you; since you cannot change it, wasting energy thinking about it or being vexed by it isn't useful. You may also find that you need to forgive the judge for interpreting the law in a way that is unfavorable to you, which will free you up to explore creative ways to work with the reality at hand.

Surprise 2. You will have to forgive everyone. Yes, everyone.

As you get closer to forgiveness, you'll find that it becomes easier as your practice becomes stronger. You'll also notice that the people around you begin to follow your lead. When you go through a divorce, you will likely feel betrayed at some stage, either by the

actual actions of your ex or by the law. While these feelings of betrayal may be the reason you've sought a divorce, or they may happen during your process, your work is to forgive it all eventually so
you can set yourself and everyone else free.

One story of betrayal that still resonates with me came from a
woman in New York City who discovered her husband was cheating on her on September 11, 2001. He'd worked in one of the towers
of the World Trade Center, and at nine fifteen that morning, she'd
called him in a panic on his cell phone asking where he was. "I'm at
my desk," he replied calmly, in the voice of a man who most definitely was not in a tower that had just been struck by an airplane.
She invited him to turn on the news. Can you imagine the roller
coaster of emotions she felt at that moment? Forgiveness was a must
for her, forgiveness for all of it—so she could move on in her own
love and happiness.

Surprise 3. Counseling can make emotional processing easier.

During divorce cases, I encourage everyone to consider counseling; divorce can be a profoundly complicated time that can leave
you feeling isolated. Whether you're mourning the loss of your family construct, confronting guilt, shame, fear, anger, sadness, irrita-
tion, impatience, self-judgment, frustration, or resentment, to have
a trained professional to guide your process can be positively transformative. Just as you would with a babysitter for your children, be sure
to keep researching and exploring until you find someone who is suitable for you and your family. A solid clinician can guide you through
this trauma by helping you release your anger so you can move forward and forgive. If verbal processing doesn't suit you, consider therapy that isn't talk-based. Eye movement desensitization reprocessing
(EMDR) and Emotional Freedom Technique (EFT) are both physi-

cal strategies that have been very useful in trauma recovery. Divorce is definitely a trauma. The sooner you begin to treat it that way, the sooner you can put it in the past. Your life is now. Treat it that way.

Surprise 4. Forgiveness is not your final step.

Now, a twist: For all the attention we've given it, forgiveness is actually just a portal for compassion, the ultimate goal. That's what will keep you moving ever forward into your greatest light, courage, and strength.

Lisa came to me a few years ago, extremely frustrated with her then-husband. Jack was simultaneously incredibly intelligent and highly immature; in Lisa's words, she had four children instead of three. When Jack failed to pay the mortgage on time, Lisa decided she wanted a divorce. Before filing for divorce, with my guidance, she'd promised herself she'd remain committed to being elegant and authentic throughout the proceedings. Together they agreed to keep their divorce out of court through peaceful attorney-assisted mediation.

The biggest obstacle for Lisa was her own mind. When she found herself criticizing him ruthlessly in her mind, she practiced shifting her focus to the ways in which she had once respected him—his intelligence, his wit, his charm. She adopted a simple, short daily meditation practice, which helped her tap into patience as the process wore on. Lisa listed what she perceived to be his most draining and frustrating qualities, and the consequences he'd suffered as a result.

Her work with me helped her gain clarity on her stance, and seeing Jack's limitations more clearly helped her begin to forgive him. She also began to see her own incapacity to find lightness and humor, and sought personal counseling to help herself find love again in the future.

At one mediation session during which we began sorting the custody details, Jack calmly stated that he actually did more than half of the work in taking care of the kids and should therefore have them the majority of the time. He loved his children, of course, but from Lisa's perspective, she was the force of the family, arranging and managing all. For her, hearing him claim that he was the primary parent felt like a sharp betrayal. As Jack's words sunk in, Lisa felt herself becoming enraged.

When something blocks your path to forgiveness

Let's take a brief time-out from Lisa's story to look more closely at what's happening. Most divorces have infinite moving parts as well as potential obstructions to forgiveness. Despite our best intentions, we may react to these obstacles in a way that prevents us from moving forward constructively. Common obstacles abound, and I'll list some here to help you recognize them before it's too late.

Discovering a prior betrayal by your ex

Hearing your ex's false claims in court or during a mediation meeting

Feeling the limitations of your weakened finances for the first time due to your legal bills

Finding out you will have to share what's yours, such as your pension or your family inheritance

Back to Lisa and Jack's mediation. As I noticed Lisa's face turning red, I requested a short break to another room. Lisa spent some quality time calming herself, hands on heart, breathing. She drank some water, used the restroom, and reminded herself that she was committed to compassion for the benefit of herself and her children. By the time she went back into negotiations, she was able to respond rather than react. We didn't settle Lisa's entire case that afternoon, of course, but Lisa avoided reacting in a manner that could have derailed or significantly delayed her divorce process.

Lisa and Jack's meetings progressed, and she was able to stay as positive as possible. To our relief and contentment, Jack followed her lead. They ultimately reached an acceptable resolution for custody, still in place in their households. Lisa and Jack attend their kids' school events together, and sometimes spend holidays as a family with their new partners. Even better, the divorce took only seven months, and they saved many thousands of dollars. My point is this: In those small moments where your ex, their attorney, or even the judge says or does something that seems patently untrue, unjust, or unforgivable, take a step back. Use every practice here to return your own body to a more positive, forgiving state. The future of your family depends on it.

And when you don't choose to forgive

Henry wanted to surprise his wife, Samantha, and their children with a dinner out one night. He came home early, while the twins were still in school, but Samantha's study was empty. Henry found her in bed with his best friend's wife, Jodi. So passionate was their encounter that they didn't hear Henry in the hallway or notice when he opened the door. The next week, Samantha was served court papers.

This was the first time Samantha had been with anyone outside of her marriage, much less a woman, which was confusing for her—but she hadn't necessarily intended to end her marriage. She begged him to come home. But Henry had put up a wall, and it was not coming down. The kids were so young that they barely remember life prior to the divorce. Without exposure to these principles, feeling betrayed, wronged, and ashamed, Henry kept his distance and committed to never talking to her again.

Samantha saw things differently. She wanted to talk about what happened and apologize, knowing it would be better for their family. The lawyers arranged a parenting schedule in which all pickups and drop-offs were at school, with minimal contact between Henry and Samantha going forward. Henry never considered forgiveness as a concept for himself or Samantha, and lived the ensuing years negative and discontented.

Surprise 5. Forgiveness takes fortitude, but grants you more strength.

In certain circles, cultures, and traditions, forgiveness is seen as a weak position, an act of giving in. You may be surprised to learn that forgiveness takes great emotional resilience. Forgiveness and its consequence, compassion, require your full attention and effort, moment by moment. It's a daily practice of tapping into a source of deep, lasting, and positive power, which both requires strength but also gives you strength.

Forgiveness also renders you completely independent from the other person. This means that, yes, you can forgive a narcissist (roughly half of my clients believe they've married a clinical narcissist) just as efficiently as you can forgive anyone else. You do not need anyone else's participation to forgive; forgiveness is the gift you give to yourself.

Surprise 6. Forgiveness comes more easily when we remember that all of this began because of love.

As difficult as it may be, remember that this relationship likely began because two humans sought and found love. It ended because one or both were not receiving that love or had found it elsewhere. It's all about love, and you're both completely and utterly human. Forgive yourself and your ex for being human, for wanting and seeking love. Even if you know things could have been handled much more appropriately, ethically, or intelligently, we all operate in our own system, with our own tools. Not everyone will read this book, and my hope is that you'll share what you're learning so more of us can be exposed to the radical idea that forgiveness and compassion are crucial to our social evolution as a species.

Surprise 7. Compassion for yourself is everything.

Once you've forgiven yourself for your role in the demise of your relationship, you will likely begin to truly start to see the world around you with greater compassion. Whether you need to forgive your blindness or your inattention, your infidelity or your incompetence, begin now. Compassion for yourself is a superpower, making even the most confusing and harrowing moments feel like an adventure shared with a dear and trusted ally—who happens to be you.

CHAPTER 7

Need-to-Know Divorce Basics

The Elegant Approach

> When two people decide to get a divorce, it isn't a sign that they "don't understand" one another, but a sign that they have, at last, begun to.
> —HELEN ROWLAND, AMERICAN HUMORIST

First, smile. Then take a deep, nourishing breath, pause a moment there, and exhale it. Now that you have explored the five essential elements in order to familiarize yourself with what is possible in your separation process, let's take a deeper look at some practical considerations as you move forward into your future. Even if you're notoriously clearheaded and calm, navigating your divorce can present the ultimate confrontation—both within yourself and with others. Let's first explore your options and determine whether you actually need to go to court. We'll also examine the selection of an attorney and discuss the role of a lawyer in your process.

Remember to be kind—most important, to yourself. The stakes

are high, because your attitude and your choices right now are the building blocks of the life you're going to be living five or ten years from now. Treat yourself and others with patience, respect, clarity, peace, and forgiveness. My favorite Italian idiom serves us well here: *Piano piano si va lontano* (Slowly, slowly one goes far). Take your time and design your approach to life every day as you proceed.

First Things First: Getting Started

Before you file for a divorce, here are three basic tenets:

1. Learn the types of divorce proceedings available in your state. Possibilities include litigation (lawsuit), mediation, lawyer-assisted mediation, and Collaborative Law.

2. Determine which approach will suit both you and your spouse.

3. Consult an attorney. If you've been served with a summons for divorce, you must consult with a lawyer to avoid inadvertently waiving your rights or missing any important deadlines. Even if your plan is to keep your family's process out of court (more on that to come), it's still intelligent to have an attorney advising you. Why? With an attorney who knows the laws in your state, you'll be able to negotiate from a place of strength and knowledge.

Remember, just because you have a lawyer doesn't mean you'll greedily fight for every penny you're entitled to receive. Together, you and your attorney can work toward a suitable agreement with open eyes and complete knowledge. Navigating a divorce is difficult enough, and with a carefully selected attorney as your partner and guide, you'll be supported even if mediation is your ultimate path to resolution. You'll also minimize your feeling of being victimized by the process.

Divorce, American Style

Years ago, the only way to resolve your divorce was by heading into court and filing an action as if you were two strangers who'd had a car accident. There is nothing family-oriented or psychologically or emotionally sensitive about the traditional classical divorce, resolved with no creativity via a stressful, angry process. While many people still choose to execute their divorce this way, today there are other options. This is the perfect crash course on what's possible for a more civilized parting.

Litigation

In this super-traditional process, each spouse is represented by a lawyer who zealously advocates for their interests. This approach can take three avenues:

BEST-CASE LITIGATION SCENARIO: Proceedings take place behind closed doors and court proceedings between the lawyers and couple. This is collaborative with a small *c*. If you're lucky enough to finally agree, the final judgment is then taken to a judge or other official, such as a hearing officer, for approval.

MOST TYPICAL SCENARIO: You reach an impasse on certain issues, so your divorce is taken to a judge to decide. At any time during this proceeding, you'll still have the opportunity to come to an agreement between yourselves, and, in fact, judges encourage it. Ultimately unless you two can agree on terms, the judge determines the outcome of your separation.

WORST CASE, AND MOST RARE SCENARIO: The divorce is contentious and emotionally raw, so the case is sent to trial in which a judge (not a jury) rules the outcome. When hostility, anger, bitterness, and other negative emotions rule, the issues that matter the most to you have the potential to end up in jeopardy. When I worked in the New York State Supreme Court for Judge Jeffrey Sunshine, he'd listen to the arguments before him in the courtroom and then ask, "Do you want this stranger in black robes deciding your life?" Often it only takes one appearance before a judge for couples to come to the realization that this isn't the way to go. Litigation often drains a family's financial resources, sometimes including college funds and savings accounts. Combative, litigious divorces always have casualties. Avoid this when possible.

Under certain circumstances, however, litigation is necessary. Some spouses are so focused on the fight that they cannot be swayed; other times, the differences are so dire that the lawyers have no choice but to appear in court. Litigation may be your only recourse to get a clear, unequivocal decision when important matters such as child custody, division of assets, and alimony are in heavy dispute. Should this happen to you, your biggest asset is still your graceful composure. Keep up with the five elements we've outlined, and hold yourself well. You can control only one aspect of this situation: your own behavior. Be clear in your thinking and as elegant as you can be in your actions. Thankfully, while sometimes court is necessary, divorces for the vast majority of families are ultimately resolved with attorneys or a mediator.

An agreement that will best suit and satisfy everyone's needs can be created only with your active input, so get involved. Your lawyer is there to offer guidance and counsel with your best interests at heart, but, in the end, you and your spouse create the terms. Remember that once you choose court, everything changes. You may hope that the judge will hear "the truth" and do what's fair, but in the typical court scenario, a judge's version of your family's future won't fully satisfy anyone. Why?

A judge who rules on your divorce is supposed to dispassionately decide issues of law and to fashion a functional agreement (decision or order) based on the facts of your case as presented. A fair-minded judge will do her or his best to accommodate your family's personal needs, but it's highly unlikely that all the nuances of your future life will be accommodated. The judge's primary responsibilities are to determine what's best for your children, and to unravel the financial entanglements that have been created. (S)he might catch some of the smaller details such as visitation for Dad on Tuesdays so Mom can work late, but even the most visionary judges don't have the ability to address every detail of your family's lifestyle. In mediation, there's a much greater chance of approaching those subtleties with care and creativity.

Note that there are some courts around the country (including Hampshire County, Massachusetts, where I practice) that are piloting successful less aggressive litigation alternatives for people for mid-level conflict cases. Before deciding to litigate on the traditional track, it is worthwhile to inquire locally to see whether your court offers any such programs.

Mediation

Mediation is now becoming the norm in the world of divorce law. This innovative approach places the choices for your future in *your* hands, not in the judgment of the stranger in black robes. Mediation can be less costly, both emotionally and financially, than litigation. In its purest form, mediation is completely client-driven, without consideration of what constraints or benefits the law could actually impose on you. It's also a very civil approach, so that your precious financial resources, including college funds and savings accounts, have the greatest chance of being spared.

Mediation involves the use of an impartial third party to help you arrive at an agreement. You and your spouse will sit with a trained mediator to tease out the particulars of your case. It is not the mediator's job to educate you about divorce law; be sure to educate yourself, preferably with the help of a lawyer who can serve as a guide on the sidelines.

Your mediator's sole responsibility is to provide a safe space in which (s)he facilitates discussions between you and your spouse. Your mediator is not here to answer your questions concerning divorce laws. A good mediator will help you address the important topics in your case and may even make suggestions, but he or she will not advise you on what you should do, nor on what would happen should you land in court. This is precisely why you need to learn the law prior to mediating. Once you're clear on your objectives, the mediator will further assist you in drafting a comprehensive agreement, which will serve as the template for your divorce settlement.

MEDIATION MYTH NO. 1. MEDIATION SAVES MONEY BECAUSE I DON'T NEED TO HIRE A LAWYER. While technically you may not *need* an attorney, it is still a good idea to use a lawyer for several reasons. At minimum, you'll need to consult with an attorney. That lawyer can instruct you about the applicable laws in your state, help you design the best way to approach your agreement, and review the final documents that will become your final dissolution contract. Depending on how much assistance you need throughout your process, your lawyer may be more hands-on.

While you'll pay for the mediator and potentially your lawyers in scheduled mediation sessions and agreement review, at least you won't be paying for those two lawyers and their hours of document drafting and endless waiting time in court.

Even with attorneys, typically with mediation financial resources will likely be conserved. And, even if mediation becomes costly or unpleasant, it is practically always going to be less emotionally damaging than litigation in the long run.

MEDIATION MYTH NO. 2. I DON'T NEED MY LAWYER TO COME WITH ME TO MEDIATION. In some cases I advise and suggest that both parties bring their lawyers to negotiate the most efficacious agreement in the shortest possible amount of time. Your mediation-friendly attorney can keep the process on track and address nuances that may or may not work in the long term. And if your spouse has a tendency to get under your skin or try to manipulate the situation, your lawyer can advocate for you and help you keep the peace within yourself and with others in the room.

MEDIATION MYTH NO. 3. IT REQUIRES BOTH PARTIES TO BE AB-SOLUTELY IN AGREEMENT AND PEACEFUL AT ALL TIMES. No, it just requires that you're both willing to do this in a more civil, open space rather than in a courtroom with a stranger who's rushing to the next case. Mediation isn't necessarily perfect, but it's way more cost-effective (financially and emotionally) and visionary than the courts.

Collaborative Divorce

While lawyers are often collaborative, there is a particular approach to family law known as Collaborative—with a capital *C*.

Collaborative refers to an intentional commitment to stay out of court. Collaborative Divorce means playing nice, commencing with the divorcing couple signing a sworn affidavit stating their intention to come to a lawyer-assisted divorce settlement that avoids intervention by a judge. That's the main characteristic of a Collaborative Divorce. The judge is not a factor—just the divorcing couple and their attorneys.

This approach requires each party to hire a lawyer trained in Collaborative Law, both of whom also sign similar statements in which they agree to work together in harmony, even if and when the two sides disagree on an issue. They also commit to following a certain set of procedures and rules. In addition, the parties agree not to discuss the case outside of the meeting room.

After the requisite agreements are signed, the couple and their lawyers come to the table with a preset agenda of elements to address one by one. The setting is designed to be informal and relaxed so all can focus and talk through an innovative solution to each aspect of your process.

Depending on the state in which you live, others may be brought in to facilitate the collaborative process, creating a team approach that some families find useful and efficient. Examples of other professionals who can facilitate an easy process: a financial planner to counsel on distribution of assets; a parenting coordinator to offer expertise in a creative parenting plan; a divorce coach to help everyone stay graceful and receptive. In my experience, these added players are often necessary, especially in cases where parenting plans are contentious and financial entanglements are complicated.

I find that couples who undergo a Collaborative Divorce experience more emotional freedom. Rather than being locked into the rules of evidence, you're just two people talking and creating agreements together with your attorneys. This approach also offers more protection than mediation, because two complementary lawyers are guiding the process.

Is there a downside to Collaborative Divorce? Yes. You may not have any way to enforce the terms of your agreement while negotiations are still in progress, as it is typically not filed with the court until all the ink is dry. There needs to be a basic level of trust and goodwill for this process to work. Also, despite considerable effort, sometimes in this process the two sides fail to agree, in which case each side will need to retain new attorneys. According to protocol (outlined in your signed agreement), your Collaborative Law attorney may not take your case to court, no matter how well your lawyer may have been working on your behalf. Pursuant to the original agreement, the parties and lawyers agree that these lawyers are disallowed from going to court if the collaboration should break down. The reason for this? You never want the Collaborative Divorce lawyer to say, "Either do this, or I am filing."

In this field, there is so much threatening that happens. By eliminating this option, the lawyers are charged to stay on track to resolution. If that doesn't happen, new attorneys are brought in. Also, it's important that both sides agree on the timelines so the resolution doesn't drag on, which can happen without court dates to drive the process.

Collaborative Divorce with a Small *C*

Sometimes, better than Collaborative Divorce, you can still have an informal "collaborative divorce" (with a small *c*). This is my favorite way to proceed. Technically it's litigation, but with two attorneys who are vested in resolution outside of court. Like Elena, if you and your spouse can find two attorneys who work well together, you can have a collaborative divorce without having to sign away your rights to litigation should you hit a snag.

Avoid "Agreements to Agree"

In an effort to hasten the divorce, the one risk of mediated agreements is that mediators are sometimes inclined to fashion agreements with unclear, noncommittal language. Such "agreements to agree" can lead to conflict and may be impossible to enforce.

For example, sometimes I see language stating that the parents "believe they can work out a holiday schedule." This is not an intelligent way to proceed, as you will have no fallback position in case of conflict. In another example, let's say your separation agreement states that your spouse has primary physical custody of your children, so you've agreed that your parenting time is "open and reasonable." While this may feel good in the moment, all too often this language turns out to be too vague and likely will lead to future conflicts. For instance, you may find yourself in a relationship with someone your ex doesn't like, and he then disallows you from seeing your children at all.

While you may avoid some difficult conversations during your mediation, this is the best time to dig in and get specific. If you wait until there is a problem to address issues, you may find yourself in court long after your mediated agreement is finalized. You may be stuck with little recourse, waiting months to see your kids as you want to due to an overcrowded court calendar, with limited resources. You don't want that. Save yourself the inevitable anguish later and create a specific agreement right now that covers these details; consider the specificity to be your insurance against an uncertain future. Remember, circumstances change, remarriage happens, illnesses occur, jobs are relocated, but nothing negates an amicable agreement more quickly than a parenting dispute. I'll get into this in more detail in chapter 9. But first let's explore the legal process a bit deeper.

Reasons to Avoid Court

Even after reading all of this, you still may still feel drawn to court, with the perception that the judge will "hear the truth" and "do what's right." Before filing in court, as mentioned previously, take time to consider whether court ensures you a better outcome. Here are a few matters to keep in mind.

Mischaracterization and courtroom humiliation are hard to scrub from your memory. Even in the best-case scenarios, a courtroom divorce is typically fraught with stress, intensity, anxiety, and raw emotions. Your lawyer may say what (s)he feels is necessary within the bounds of the law to get you what you feel you deserve. Then your spouse's lawyer gets to retaliate, usually with a reworked version of the same story; now you are the villain, not your spouse. Facts get twisted, doubts regarding integrity and stability are raised, parenting skills are challenged, and deeply personal matters are openly discussed in the courtroom. This whole process will likely leave you with memories you'd rather avoid.

It's also going to cost you—a lot. Going to court drains away your money, your time, and your personal dignity. Once you enter the courtroom, privacy is left at the door. In court, typically there are no real winners. In addition to lost time from work and diminished dignity, litigation is typically the most expensive way to get a divorce. Legal fees, typically starting at hundreds of dollars per hour, add up quickly. Preparing various statements, documents, and depositions—not to mention sitting in meetings and hearings—

takes many hours, costing you tens of thousands of dollars. On top
of that, you can spend half the day sitting around in the courthouse
waiting for your ten minutes in front of the judge. Sometimes, even
after all the waiting, the judge may not make a decision during your
first court appearance, and you'll likely have to come back several
times to provide even more information, which adds to your costs.
The bottom line is that court comes with its own timeline and procedures. Litigated cases often run into five figures (sometimes even six
figures), especially in larger cities and communities where there are
usually longer court waiting times and higher hourly fees.

There are limits to what you can present in court. Sometimes
people want to go to court because they've been so deceived or feel
so victimized that they think the judge naturally would side with
them. Realistically, this is not typical at all. There are limits to what
a judge will agree to hear, and the law dictates what information
the judge can hear. Additionally, your lawyer has to follow certain
rules of evidence, meaning anything that can be described as hear-
say (for example, "my kids said this happened" and "this person told
me that he said that") is off the table. Even though you feel it should
matter that your spouse's girlfriend is already pregnant and flaunts
it in front of your kids, it may not hold much weight from a legal
perspective.

What the judge hears in the short time you're actually in the
courtroom is typically a small slice of your story. Even if the issues
you deem noteworthy do get brought up in court, this does not
mean the judge's decision will be based on those issues. The perceived injustices and grievances that matter most to you and your
family are often not admissible and won't factor into the court's
decision. The law is designed to deal with legally relevant facts, not
emotional issues.

The court may never address the small stuff. If you think a judge is going to resolve petty grievances over such things as who gets your aunt Anna's antique crystal bowl, you're mistaken. As Judge Sunshine was fond of saying, "I don't do tchotchkes!" Tchotchkes is an old Yiddish word for the small trinkets that we sometimes keep for posterity. If the two of you can't work out the small matters yourself, you could end up paying several court-appointed professionals such as lawyers or an arbitrator to help you sort it all out. You may wind up paying them more than the value of the stuff you are fighting over.

Even after your day in court, you may still not feel validated. I've often heard people complain about experiencing a hurried vibe from people in the judicial system. For example, betrayed spouses may see court as a forum to vent their anger on a cheating spouse in public, only to discover that the court doesn't deem that important. Why? Although such matters are emotionally complicated, infuriating, and important, they are typically not legally relevant. Consider the story told earlier about the woman who learned her husband who worked in one of the towers at the World Trade Center was clueless as to the attack, as he was cheating on her on the morning of September 11. Since this story is highly unlikely to shock a judge, or greatly impact the outcome of your case, you may be better off processing your emotions and spending your money with a good therapist.

JUDGES ARE ONLY HUMAN. Judges are not wizards with superpowers. They hear dozens of cases a week, and nothing you say about what your spouse did is likely to surprise them or sway them into making your case an exception. Their responsibility is to consider the facts as presented, rather than the emotions, and make decisions consistent with the statutes and case law in their jurisdiction. Hard as it may be to hear, most of the time in divorce law there is no objectively right outcome. Even if the laws were uniform state to state, strict guidelines inform the law, but each judge interprets the law differently. The facts of a case are filtered through the judge's point of view, background, life experiences, and even their mood that day. The bottom line is that if you go to trial, you aren't necessarily going to like the result, and you have no choice but to live with it.

Elena chose to stay far away from court.

At that time, my son's dad and I knew that we wanted to get our divorce sorted as efficiently as possible and move forward as friends. We each retained a lawyer, and he generously paid the retainer for both of the lawyers. We drafted a document that contained the points we each wished to cover, super factually, and met with both attorneys twice, once to finish drafting and once to sign it. It wasn't perfect, and implementing it wasn't always easy. Like most of us reading this, we both thought we were the one for each other at a certain time. But seeing each other as co-parent, as friend, and as family, we got through it. The two lawyers we'd hired have worked together before, and there was even laughter in the conference room during signing. We were committed and intentional, and we proudly crafted an agreement that's served us well.

Things to Remember If You Find Yourself in Court

SOMETIMES COURT IS NECESSARY. Occasionally, filing with the court is the only way to get your partner to engage in the process, in the cases where one side is actively avoiding it. In certain cases, you may need to protect yourself from a spouse who is trying to freeze you out of assets. Perhaps your spouse is stubborn or simply misinformed about what going to court entails. Maybe your ex is attempting to alienate you from your children. If you do find yourself in court, focus on the positive aspects and do your best to create a reasonable resolution anywhere along the way. You can still hold the ideal of creating a better future as you courageously take on the litigation experience. Take heart, the vast majority of cases settle prior to trial. By incorporating the elements of patience, respect, clarity, peace, and forgiveness, you will emerge from this process with ease and grace.

PRIORITIZE DIGNITY. Regardless of what brought your case to court, you must choose to proceed with dignity. Shift your energy in the direction of clear, compassionate, focused, and mindful thinking by using the practices you've learned. Your embodiment of grace as you go through this process will make your life better after your divorce. And while you may not get everything you were hoping for, the energy you bring to the courtroom will come through and serve you as you move forward.

HOLD YOUR GROUND. Don't let the enormity of a public hearing intimidate you into giving away what fairly should be yours. Take time to consider both factually and intuitively when something important is at stake, and hold your ground if necessary. When a remark or assumption gets under your skin, employ the mindfulness techniques from earlier in this book. And don't forget to keep your body well and moving, so you can be strong and soft in equal measures.

Remember, you may still shift out of court at any point . . . even if you begin there, you may typically opt out at any time. If the possibility of resolution arises, there is more room for compromise than you might think. Be observant, listen carefully to what is being

said, and stay curious. See if you can find a place where agreement
and cooperation emerge.

Finding the Right Attorney and Communicating Your Needs

Your lawyer should be intelligent, adaptable, and savvy—and a
strong negotiator. Your lawyer should be open-minded, direct, eth-
ical, and compassionate, and should support you while taking into
account your entire family's needs and be candid about what you
can expect. Your lawyer should also be willing to help you swiftly
dissolve your marriage outside the courtroom. Perhaps most important, be certain that this person has a sense of humor. How will
you find such a lawyer?

ASK AROUND. Talk to people who've been divorced, inquire about
their experience, and ask for recommendations. You could also consult with your local bar association about attorneys in your area who
specialize in divorce. When you ask why they are recommending
a specific person, listen for descriptions such as direct, personable,
likable, smart, savvy, fair, diligent, honest, compassionate, patient,
or a good listener.

Then check their reputation. Most divorce lawyers, especially
those who have been around for a while, end up recognized for a
certain style. I have a reputation for being a little unconventional
and resolving my cases quickly—an iron fist in a velvet glove. I'm
notably no-nonsense, casual, and super clear in my work. Clients
often come into my office crying and leave laughing. I try to keep it
as light as possible, and I am here to safeguard both their financial
and emotional welfare as I advocate for them. And a note of caution:
While you do want a lawyer who can be tough, beware of the ag-

gressive, take-no-prisoners bulldog who can potentially cause your family unanticipated damage. For some divorce lawyers, the primary goal is the win. Your well-chosen lawyer will seek an efficient resolution for your whole family.

CONDUCT A PRELIMINARY INTERVIEW. Some lawyers will give you ten to fifteen minutes of free or reduced-rate phone time to answer some preliminary questions and to assess their working style. Remember, you're hiring, this is your divorce, and this person is going to help you design your future. During that quick conversation you can accomplish a few simple goals, listed here. If you're willing to consider them to represent you, I'll give you more specific questions to ask in the next section.

MAKE SURE THEY SPECIALIZE IN DIVORCE LAW. Remember, just because someone is at a big firm doesn't mean they're skilled in family law. Corporate lawyers may be brilliant, but they likely don't understand how to finesse a family law case. Those who engage specifically in family practice have experience and skill. Criminal lawyers are typically more inclined to go for the win. A real estate attorney may see your divorce as primarily transactional. Any of these practitioners might do a fine job, but your money and time are best spent on someone whose daily practice focuses on family law.

VERIFY YOUR COMPATIBILITY. Ask how quickly you can expect return calls or emails. Your lawyer should be available to you and open to your needs; he or she should buy into your goal to resolve quickly. Which leads to our next point to touch on during your first talk.

ENSURE THEIR OPENNESS TO MEDIATION OR TO WORK COLLABORATIVELY. This one is exceedingly important, so be specific and crystal clear. The attorney you select must be open-minded about mediation or collaborative lawyering—period. Some lawyers want to keep their clients on the traditional litigation track, and many see agreeability as counterproductive to proper representation. Mediation typically means the lawyer will earn less from you, so be sure you're clear as you begin.

CONFIRM THEIR INTEREST IN SUPPORTING YOUR FAMILY'S WELL-BEING DURING THE DIVORCE. At the start, clearly state outright your own version of what you're seeking. "I'm not interested in going to battle with my spouse. I want to be respectful, patient, peaceable, and make decisions and suggestions with clarity. And while I'm not there yet, my aim is full forgiveness." Notice their response and see if it resonates with your goals.

Your Initial Legal Consultation

If your preliminary conversation goes well, you may choose to "interview" that person to be your attorney. It is typically worth the money to interview at least two attorneys to see who's best to guide you through your process intelligently as part of your team. Once you've found an attorney with whom you can consider moving forward, here's what to keep in mind as you begin your initial legal consultation.

LEARN THE LAWS IN YOUR STATE. This first meeting is your opportunity to learn your rights in your jurisdiction or state. Please highlight the following sentence. Do *not* rely on what your friends tell you, and do not rely on what you read online about the laws in your state. Only your carefully chosen lawyer knows the nuances of the laws, courts, and judges where you live. Only that person can give proper and useful insight into the particular facts of your case as they may play out in court.

ASK SPECIFIC QUESTIONS. When you meet with your prospective lawyer, weave the following into your introductory conversation:

What is your experience with family law?

How many of your cases resolve without court intervention?

What is your hourly rate? (A note of caution here: An attorney with a low hourly rate may be less experienced, less efficient, or bill more aggressively for every interaction, copy, or email than their pricier counterpart, and ultimately the bottom line is identical.)

How long will it take for me to get divorced if I file?

How does custody work in this state? Can I leave the state with my child(ren) during the divorce?

Will I receive/have to pay child support?

If I choose to move out of the house, what are the consequences?

Does it matter in this state who files first?

How does asset division work in this state (what is marital, what is separate)?

How is debt allocated? What is marital and who has to pay them?

Would I receive or owe spousal support (aka maintenance/ alimony)?

How does health insurance work?

How might a judge respond in this state if I remove money from our joint account before filing?

How do we handle the marital home?

What happens to my (my spouse's) inheritance?

Who gets the kids on the holidays?

How can we resolve this with the greatest ease?

TAKE GOOD NOTES. This first meeting is a simple fact-finding mission. Prior to the meeting, gather as much information as you can about your assets, including retirement plans, insurance plans, and liabilities. Listen carefully, take good notes, and, most important, ask questions. You are the client, and you're likely going to get a second opinion. No matter how compelling this person is, you are the one "shopping," so ask a lot of questions.

CHECK IN WITH YOUR GUT. I am an advocate of trusting your own intuition, so if the first lawyer feels right to you, go for it. If you hire an attorney and it starts to get a little rocky, however, try to stick it out—firing your lawyer suggests you may be the difficult one, especially if you end up also firing lawyer number two. That said, if you feel you've made a mistake in your choice of a lawyer, seek a second opinion. Then, when it feels right, cut your losses and move on. This may add to your expenses, but it's far better than regretting your settlement after the fact.

CONSIDER A LAWYER FOR YOUR SPOUSE. Ideally, you and your spouse will hire lawyers who like each other and have worked together well in the past. If your spouse has yet to hire a lawyer, you should also use this first meeting to discuss who might be a good lawyer to represent him or her. Even if you and your spouse totally disagree on most things, this strategy works best for everyone trying to arrive at amicable terms. Of course, the more amicable you and your spouse are, the smoother the process and better the outcome is likely to be. Elena and her son's dad did this and were happy with their fast, amicable process. A lot of people are surprised when I say this, as most think the typical process involves two lawyers who will fight for their clients like they do on television. In real life, that sort of environment only creates stress, bad feelings, and unfortunate memories. Two opposing lawyers who are familiar with each other's styles and skills can help make the process smooth and relatively quick.

Elena's story is a good example of finding a lawyer who supports the ideals of a healthy, peaceful divorce.

Elena's Story: The Right Lawyer Makes a Difference

My son's dad and I had a unique story, in that we knew from the start that we wanted a fast, smooth resolution to our chapter as a married couple. He found me a lawyer who was a close colleague of his lawyer, knowing that we would be handling each other and our process with care. In our case, we didn't need a mediator because we were on the same page with regard to the particulars of our divorce. I could say we were lucky, but I believe we create our own fortune via our behavior. And while I wasn't perfect the whole way through, our objective to accomplish this separation with grace led us both through it.

Sitting down in that first meeting, I felt at ease because I'd invited my best friend and business partner to come along, helping me feel comfortable and safe. I'd strongly recommend bringing someone who can be present and stable for you so you're never feeling alone in your process. At that first meeting I reiterated to my lawyer our shared intention: to arrive at our agreement amicably and smoothly. I remember feeling quite clear that day. I was definitely nervous, struggling to stay present, but my overarching intent was my buoy on a rough ocean. Almost immediately upon stating that financially, I'd ask only for what was absolutely necessary, the resonance in the room changed. Within weeks we were divorced and signing papers at a subsequent meeting, exchanging caring, trusting smiles. We've been helping each other and creating a functional family ever since.

CHAPTER 8

Don't Let Money Move You

Defining Your Emotions, Desires, and Needs

An investment in knowledge pays the best interest.
—BENJAMIN FRANKLIN

Before we begin exploring your post-separation finances, know this: once your money matters are sorted, your life will fall into place. The five principles will help you gain momentum to move forward, and your commitment to begin with your eyes and mind wide open to being factual about money will be extremely beneficial to you and your family.

Even if you have plenty of material wealth, graciously parting with what once belonged to you will likely be difficult at first. Splitting assets along with income and debt allocation can be troublesome, particularly when it feels like there isn't enough to go around. The goal? To emerge from your divorce with precisely what you need to move your life forward with a feeling of prosperity and even abundance. Most of the puzzle is learning how to part with what you don't truly need, which helps open the internal space to feel complete. And if that sounds crazy to you, read on.

Many of my clients feel overwhelmed when I share the financial disclosure statement with them; this is where I have them fill me in on all the assets, liabilities, and matters of finance that pertain to their partnership. But once they start fact-finding, learning and writing it all down, many report that this aspect of the process is actually a clarifying and edifying endeavor. Over time, many appreciate the value of this process, as it helps them to become more comfortable and savvy with regard to finances.

Combating Inertia

You can make smart choices only with a robust understanding of your finances. What exactly does that mean? An awareness of the money coming in, money owed, value of personal property, real estate, investment portfolios, and retirement accounts. As you begin exploring these financial aspects of your divorce, you may find yourself filled with emotion, attachment, and fear. This is your opportunity to start shifting this paradigm of overwhelm around finances—you're not alone. Here are some reminders of these five elemental awarenesses as we enter into the territory of finances, nobody's favorite. This is a big area of potential healing for all of us.

Patience

Splitting assets can take time and possibly several focused sessions with your lawyer or in mediation. Retirement plans, businesses, property, and valuable items are all part of the consideration, so many details need to be covered. As you begin to figure out what's at stake, what you want, and what you need, aim to leave each negotiating session having made a tiny bit of progress. Every small step counts.

Respect

Relinquishing some of the material marital assets out of sheer respect for your past may actually help you to release residual negative energy. If you find yourself in a stalemate over some object like the TV, the blender, or the vacuum cleaner, opt to let that object go in order to focus on respectful compromise and forward momentum. When at least one party comes to the table with respect, discussions over material items can more efficiently be crossed off the list.

Clarity

Set aside time to carefully consider what you need going forward. Keep focused on the difference between your needs and your desires; you began that list in the chapter on clarity. When finances are being addressed, you'll have your needs clearly and specifically outlined, ready to be elegantly presented.

Peace

When it comes to finances, peace is a generous attitude, a sign of your evolution, and a wondrous example for your children. When you're at a loss, ask, "What is the most peaceful move I can make in this moment?" And when it comes to these volatile matters of money, do what you can to be reasonable, give what you can, or clearly ask for what you need, in order to invite more harmony and peacefulness into your overall process.

Forgiveness

Accept that the past cannot be changed. Forgive your part, forgive
the others in the story, so that you can free up your own momentum.
Your forgiveness forges the path for compassion, which yields creativity and resourcefulness for your whole family. In one example,
a client of mine settled and received the minimum amount for child
support, and when she began earning more than her ex, she redi-
rected the child support into her child's college fund. Forgiveness.

Moving Forward: Mine, Yours, or Ours?

Depending on where you live, there are laws regarding what is individual property versus marital property. Some states view everything
as belonging to both of you, regardless of the source or when it was
acquired. Other states take the position that ownership runs with the
title or depends on when or how it was acquired. Still others consider
assets that accumulate passively as separate (e.g., appreciated property value due to market changes), whereas accumulated assets due
to joint efforts are jointly owned (i.e., renovation). Your attorney can
help you understand the specific laws where you live.

Mike had a classic car sitting in his garage long before he married,
and during the marriage he used money from his wife, Sydney, and
their joint accounts to accomplish the restoration. By the time they
split, the car was worth ten times what he'd originally paid for it.
Her money was now in it, too, not just his. So whose car is it now?
Often even when the law actually approaches property division as
an equitable split, this phrase is always up to subjective interpretation. *Equitable* does not necessarily mean equal. Elena offers a sweet,
brief meditation for accessing that fine balance between holding on

and letting go. Your breathing is everything, and this will help you recenter and prioritize.

This meditation can be done anywhere, almost anytime (just not while you're driving!). It will help you sense where in your body you are holding tension and will help you to release it. The intention is to help you be more willing to let go of tightness in regard to your possessions, your opinions, and your assumptions.

First, take a moment to quiet down and listen to the cadence of your breathing in this moment. Dare yourself to just stop for a few minutes and let your body get still. Your breathing seems to become louder as you let the rest of the world get quiet around you; that's perfect. Notice the breath moving in through your nostrils down into your belly, and then exhale from there, emphasizing the way your belly moves toward your spine. Spend several breaths there, noticing if your body feels any tension or contraction anywhere. Continue this practice, emphasizing the navel moving back and up as you exhale, until you feel any pattern of tension or contraction dissipate. Notice now that your mind has become more still, and your thoughts have likely begun to slow down.

After a few minutes, take a moment to consider what it would feel like to let go of a possession that matters a great deal to you. When you feel your body tense up, use the breathing you've just practiced to dissolve that tension. Then try working with a long-held belief or assumption you hold about someone in your life. Again, when you notice the physical tightness, use the breathing practice to still the mind and soften the body. You may do this with a few different thoughts or things, becoming proficient at the act of releasing these items and ideas one at a time using your breathing.

On Dignity

At some point, asset splitting is likely to be—or seem—unfair. Maintaining your dignity is critical to the process of your divorce. Use the tools to stay patient, clear, respectful, peaceful, and forgiving. In a few years, when you look back, the dignity you practiced will provide a good memory. Choosing otherwise will leave traces of negativity that you won't want to bring with you as you move forward.

Refining Your Wants Versus Your Needs

In chapter 4, you created lists of wants and needs. Now that we're talking specifically about financial matters, it's time to put those lists under a microscope. Getting crystal clear on your needs increases the likelihood of fulfillment. While negotiation still happens, being clear about what you need is the first step. Given what you're now learning about division of assets, go back, if necessary, and reread chapter 4 and enlist the exercises you did then as you do your review. Consider your financial and material assets based on these criteria. Remember, when it comes to division of assets, it should all be about fairness.

Wants are emotionally based, personal, and subjective.

Needs are impersonal, objective, and based on what is right for all members of the family.

Next add two more columns next to your needs, and two more columns next to your wants. As best as you can ascertain, note the "owner" of each item according to these guidelines. Since the ownership of possessions often comes into question, unless it is clearly joint property, we will label it "questionably mine" or "questionably not mine." Remember, any prenuptial agreement you have will be the guide to these basic categories.

LEGALLY BOTH OF OURS. It's a mutually owned or marital asset, such as your house and furniture purchased with your monetary wedding gifts, or your joint savings. Remember, though, that the definition of marital asset varies from state to state, so ask your lawyer to be sure.

QUESTIONABLY MINE. You brought it into the marriage; it exists for your use only or mostly, or your spouse has no use for it.

QUESTIONABLY NOT MINE. Your spouse brought it into the marriage, *but* you need it to sustain your household and/or you can't afford to replace it. Notice there is no designation labeled "Definitely Mine" or "Definitely Not Mine"—nothing is absolute until the final agreement or judgment.

Next, in the third column, assign a monetary value to the assets; be as accurate as possible. If you own a home you need to figure out its market value. A licensed real estate appraiser is typically the preferred option but, if you have no money to spare for a licensed appraiser, at least consider having a Realtor conduct an informal appraisal before assigning a value to this asset. If you have personal property (tangible belongings other than real estate) such as antiques, fine art, and expensive jewelry, you may wish to have them appraised. We often are emotionally attached to belongings but in the division of assets they are worth quite a bit less than imagined. Remember, you are looking for resale value.

If there's an item on your list that you feel is yours but may be claimed by your spouse, gather documentation that will help prove it should belong to you, especially for items you've listed as "questionably not mine" but you feel are a "need" in your future life. This exercise is important, as it will be used to help you get clear on your financial needs. With this clarity, you and/or your attorney can do the best negotiation on your behalf.

Prepare yourself. Even if you're comfortable with numbers, engaging in this exercise can be stressful. At first especially, there may be a lot of emotion tied up in material belongings—even belongings whose value is largely sentimental. You may also be worried about how you are going to survive moving forward, or annoyed that you have to share what you perceive to be your accumulated wealth that you do not wish to share. Remember your focus is on figuring out what you need to move forward. By engaging in the five elemental practices, you will move through this as compassionately as possible. As you begin to scratch the surface of your financial picture, especially if you are feeling anxious, irritated, or blue, consider Elena's thoughts and Meditation on Abundance.

> Abundance is created from within you. With this meditation you'll create an energetic blueprint that welcomes and supports total abundance in your being and in your world. This practice takes a look at how everything evolves from the self, meaning: How are you generating this moment from within yourself? When things feel good and full, that's coming from within you. If you're feeling like there is something missing in your outer life, can you ask what you might be inventing that is missing from within you?
>
> As you sit quietly, breathing deeply and being simply aware, bring a feeling of fullness to this moment, creating a feeling of abundance within and around you. Breathe quietly

but fully, until you feel this fullness as the only reality in your body . . .

An abundance of breath. An abundance of oxygen.
An overflow of healing space within your body.
A deep well of knowing, clear love.

Practice this when you're yearning for a feeling of more fullness. Practice this when things feel scarce or scary. Practice this quiet, full breathing whenever you need to create a sensation of abundance in any realm of your life.

To enrich this sitting, spend a few silent minutes seeing your body as a mansion, a huge and beautiful mansion of many rooms. At this moment you're living in just one or two of those rooms. Begin to notice the ways in which your breathing extends to all those other far reaches of the mansion, and how truly extraordinary and exquisite those rooms are. Take a few minutes here to explore. Just notice where you go.

To create abundance is an advanced practice. See and sense a vision of how you'd like your life to be. Whatever aspect of your life is involved, spend these next few minutes holding the scene in your mind, and, more important, feeling the feeling of that abundant reality being true. What will it feel like when that is true? Receive that reality and breathe quietly and fully into it.

As you close this meditation, consider this truth, which comes from *Oneness* by Rasha. "The fact is, there is no limitation whatsoever in the structure of your fundamental essence. The key to transcending conditions in which you perceive the evidence of limitation: to dwell, utterly and completely, in a

perception of how you would like it to be." To complete your
meditation, sit quietly for as long as you wish.

Letting Go of Guilt

Some people, especially those who've somehow betrayed, cheated on,
or otherwise wronged their spouses, often feel guilty about their behavior or their choice to divorce, which compels them to give it all
away. While I always encourage generosity, if you are in this camp,
be certain that you won't regret it later. As with most strong emotions,
guilt goes away, but asset division is often final, at least in the eyes of
some courts. When I represent the betrayed or jilted party, I almost
always encourage them to take the first offer, as it tends to be the best.

Others give in and give away too much because they do not know
how to advocate for themselves. Remember, it's not greedy to take
care of yourself and have your needs met. If this feels familiar, allow me to underscore this point: Being sure your needs are met is
showing compassion toward yourself, and most likely benefits your
ex from a universal perspective. For you to be happy is good for
everyone involved. If you cannot or will not advocate for yourself,
please be certain to have a lawyer advocate for you. It's a long-term
investment in your future.

Family Finances: The Fundamentals

Prior to the 1980s, many women caught in divorce or separation
lived a second-class lifestyle, mostly because compared to men, most
women lacked access to significant earning potential and the ability

to accrue substantial retirement interest. Financially, most divorced women tended to struggle. New laws were created at that time to help even out the discrepancy between the divorcing households. In an effort to avoid creating a power imbalance, with one wealthy home and one poor home, the courts attempted to prevent extreme economic disparity between the post-divorce homes. Today, these economics are coming back to center, due to increasing numbers of two-income homes in which both parents share the care and custody of the children.

The concepts of property distribution and alimony are ever changing and vary greatly among and even within states. Today, typically, the overall ideal around asset and debt allocation is designed to create a result that fairly distributes the family's wealth as it exists at the moment of separation. Your lawyer can help you sort out what you can expect to give and take in your separation, as well as how money will flow between your households.

However, first you need to know what you own, what you owe, what you earn, and what you spend. Once you understand the flow of money through your household and the amount of debt the two of you have accumulated, you can begin to fashion a sensible plan to move forward. Here is a quick look at the four moving targets that impact your financial resolution. Remember, this is just a look at all the finances without consideration as to whether each item is separate or marital property.

Income

In addition to salary, income may also include dividends from stocks and bonds, royalties, bonus income, trust income, income from outside work, or income from rental properties. If you or your spouse doesn't work, or one or both of you are underemployed, there may also be imputed income—income attributed to you as though you were employed. Your lawyer can tell you what else may count as income in your jurisdiction.

Expenses

This covers the monthly cost of running your household, including mortgage, child care, electric and gas bills, insurance, car payments, Internet, cable, home phone, mobile phone(s), groceries, clothing, gifts, extracurricular activities, et cetera. Expenses may also include payment on any debts brought into the marriage, such as student loans, or child support or alimony being paid to a previous ex.

Assets

This includes all your valuable possessions: your home, investment property, car, airplane, boat, machinery, money in the bank (all checking and savings accounts), investments, retirement accounts (defined contribution and defined benefit), stocks, bonds, options, royalties (accrued or otherwise anticipated), household valuables that appreciate in value (such as silver, art, fine antiques, and quality collectibles), jewelry, inheritances, lottery or other betting wins, pending lawsuit awards.

Debts

This includes what's still owed, including interest, on your ongoing large-ticket items, such as a primary mortgage, a second mortgage, automobile(s), lines of credit, student or other types of loans, and items such as boats, motorcycles, coin collections, and the like.

Next, subtract your debts from your assets, and you have your net worth. To determine what portion of the net worth is yours, you'll need to consult an attorney. Unless you have a binding prenuptial agreement that imposes significant monetary limitations, many states (not all) view your entitlement after your divorce as approximately half of what it was when you married, or what is deemed equitable in your situation.

For the purposes of this example, let's say your combined net worth comes to $430,000. In theory, if all the resources are marital, depending on where you live, if you acquired everything during the marriage you may expect to each exit the marriage with up to around $215,000. Depending on the nature of the property (marital or separate) and overall income flow, you may wind up with more or less in your final resolution. You might choose to agree to less now in exchange for a larger portion in the future—or you might agree to more now (e.g., keep the house) for less in the future (e.g., waive rights to the pension). This is why you need to be prepared: it's all a negotiation, and the more clarity you have, the easier it will be to move through it.

Gather all the above information as early in the process as possible and share it with your lawyer. If you don't know what your spouse has or owes, ask. Information is power. You're entitled to know all about your spouse's finances, so if your spouse is not forthcoming, your lawyer can request the information legally.

Consider a Financial Consultant

You may wish to hire a financial planner who specializes in restructuring finances for families that are separating. A capable consultant can help you explore your options and fashion a financial plan along with your lawyer, so that you'll retain the most money for your family's needs and spend as little on taxes as possible. Applications particularly tailored for financial planners assisting families in transition may help you sort the more complex financial questions. Just be certain that your lawyer and your financial planner are transparently communicating with each other.

Possession Checklist

Before negotiating, take careful stock of your family's balance sheet. Here's a helpful checklist for you.

____ Appraisal/valuation of real estate.

____ Appraisal/valuation of business(es).

____ Value of all personal property (make a separate list for this). Other than valuables, remember that your belongings will be valued at eBay, Craigslist, or garage sale prices.

____ Value of mature stock options, pending royalties, or other anticipated earned revenue.

____ Value of all current bank and investment accounts.

____ Value of retirement accounts, pension plans, and college savings accounts, if any.

____ Value of all liabilities (total amount owed, not monthly payment amount), including mortgage, car loans, pension loans, credit card or student debt, personal loans (make a separate list for this).

____ List all credit cards and ascertain whether they are yours, your spouse's, or both. Call the credit card company, as you may not be able to tell from face of card (make a separate list for this).

____ Be sure to note whether each asset is joint or individual, and gather documentation to present in order to make this case. Your lawyer will help you determine whether an asset is considered joint or separate, according to the law in your state.

The Family Home

Deciding what happens with the marital home tends to be one of the most difficult decisions in the separation process. For many, in addition to its monetary value, there is usually significant emotional weight attached to the family home. Perhaps you found it, and your social community is located there. Maybe you've redesigned it or decorated it with exquisite care. Maybe you are concerned that if you leave the home, the kids will not feel as connected to you. And maybe, although buying out your spouse isn't realistic, downsizing or moving into a less expensive neighborhood just doesn't seem like a viable option.

So how does this play out? Fifty or more years ago, divorce for all except the wealthy pretty much meant that mom and the kids would end up living below the standard that existed during the marriage, while the dad would move forward with financial security. About thirty-five years ago, the pendulum swung in the other direction. The tide began shifting, placing the mom and the kids in the house, while the dad had to figure out how to support them from elsewhere, in a small apartment. With two working parents today, family property is part of the open playing field. In your case, if you find letting go of your house an impossible consideration, here are some economic inquiries to consider:

Can you afford to buy out your spouse (or to have your spouse buy you out) and continue to make the mortgage and maintain the house?

Can you afford to make the mortgage and maintain the house, even if resolution allows for you to retain an unequal amount of equity in the home?

Is it possible to cut back on some expenses in a way that makes keeping the house possible?

Is your spouse willing to let you and the children (or vice versa) remain in the family home and contribute to its upkeep until a predetermined time in the future, such as when the kids go to college or go off on their own?

Are you and your spouse willing and affordably able to leave the family home intact and each get your own place while trading off living with the children? This is a modern trend called nesting (covered in chapter 9).

These are just some of the viable options that can be put on the table in a negotiation. Any number of terms and agreements are possible. If your spouse is being unreasonable and the answers to all these questions is no, you don't have much of a choice but to agree to sell, take your proceeds, and find a more affordable place that works with your single salary plus any child support and/or alimony to which you might be entitled. You need to be unapologetically realistic and honest with yourself. You and the children will likely be even better with a fresh start in a new environment. Shake away assumptions that keep you feeling victimized and be willing to begin again.

You may consider continuing to co-own property if you cannot afford to buy out your partner's interest right away. Unless you're highly knowledgeable regarding such matters, disentangling your shared property is the simplest way to part. Avoiding the pain now can complicate the future, when the house needs work and money is tight. If you do decide to co-own, be sure to be very clear in your agreement regarding what you're sharing, as well as deferred maintenance as you move forward. Co-ownership can work for some separating couples, but be sure you're clear in your ongoing expectations before signing an agreement.

Elena has a practical meditation, which is actually a simple reading on the concept of home, that might help you move through this process. It's for anytime you're feeling unmoored, unsure, and unclear about where you stand. Take a moment, wherever you are, to take a few deep breaths and consider what home means to you. You may read this silently to yourself or aloud, and imbibe the words as you redefine the concept of home.

Home is not a place. Home is a state of consciousness.
Home is my forgiveness. Home is my alchemy.
Home is my promise. Home is my empathy.
Home is my humanity, and, yes, home is my family, with their crazy and
   their beauty,
And home is the creation I fashion from reality.
Home is even the illusion of separation from my highest identity.
Home is the place where I get to be evolutionary.
Home is touching, greeting, recognizing, embracing.
Home is seeing into the depths of someone else's true nature.
Home is exploring, accepting, and liberating.
Home is oneness; it's guidance, it's listening, it's stunning.
Today, I give thanks for this invitation,
this inspiration, this homecoming.

Pensions and Retirement Accounts

After twenty years of marriage, Anna and Steve came to a mutual conclusion—they'd be better apart. Without kids, they figured divorcing would be a simple process. They agreed to sell their almost-paid-for house and split the equity. They divided up their cars and other possessions evenly. There was one contentious issue: Steve had a government pension, whereas Anna had no retirement plan. Her only future financial security was Social Security. When Anna's lawyer confirmed, according the law where she lived, that she had a right to half of Steve's pension that had accumulated during their marriage, she decided she needed it. Steve, my client, was bothered, to say the least. In his mind, she'd wasted her future savings on clothing, and he wasn't happy to part with half his pension.

It may not seem fair, but I explained to him that his pension is an asset, just like the house or the bank account. Anna was legally entitled to half of what his fund had accumulated while they were married. But, I explained to him, just because she's entitled doesn't necessarily mean that he has to hand it over. We negotiated, and I had to urge him to find something else to give up.

When it comes to divorce and money, your pension may not be yours alone in the eyes of the law. Steve was adamant enough to work on keeping his, so I suggested first to determine how flexible Anna would be. As it turned out, Anna and Steve opted for mediation, with my guidance for Steve in the background. The result? Steve agreed to give Anna a larger piece in the split of their house if she'd rescind her claim to a share of his pension. It was less than she would have received in splitting the pension, but she was compensated immediately and both were satisfied.

Inheritance and Family Gifts

If you live in a state where gifts and inheritances come into the negotiations in divorce, chances are you will be advised to get a prenuptial agreement when you marry if you anticipate receiving a sizable inheritance or a family gift in the future. If an inheritance is considered marital property where you live, this means that regardless of why you separate, you may need to share at least some of it with your ex. How this works depends on both the law in your area and your judge's interpretation. If you don't have a prenuptial agreement and are expecting (or managing) any sort of inheritance, be sure to retain an attorney to ascertain your rights and obligations.

In cases including inheritances, the best advice is to practice equanimity and dignity in such matters from the start. What feels best for your family as a whole? How can we come together with a reasonable resolution for all? Elena has a short, simple sitting meditation to help you release what needs to be released, and invite abundance of all kinds for yourself and your family.

Take a seat, close your eyes, and begin to pay attention to your breathing. The moment you go inside, you'll notice a feeling of expansion, a sensation of opening. Stay with that for a few breaths. Now begin to deepen your breathing, and invite your inhalation to reach all the way to the perimeter of your body, your skin. Exhale fully, letting all the air out, your belly moving back toward your spine. Next, inhale even more fully, as though you could extend your breath past the boundary of your skin, and hold it in for a moment. Feel that fullness. Then exhale, bringing your navel back and up, to release the breath out. Notice the quiet, the stillness, and the peace there.

With each passing breath, you have a chance to experience the fullness internally, to savor it, and then to let it go. This is an articulate way to look at all of your possessions, even the things that hold great meaning for you. You can take a full moment to experience the meaning, the richness, the depth—of the item, the relationship—but in letting it go, you can also experience a new freedom and a new space to be filled with something even more fulfilling and enriching. Sit quietly and entertain this fullness until you feel that you've shifted into a state of more equanimity.

Child Support: What That Means Today

Unless you both earn an equal amount of money and share the exact same amount of time with your kids, there is a reasonable likelihood that one of you will be paying to help support the kids. However, as with all laws pertaining to marriage and family, the structure of child support is based on the laws in the state and jurisdiction in which you live.

Typically, child support is based on a formula that considers the parties' incomes; the number of children; the allocation of time between the parents; medical, dental, and child care expenses; and any amounts paid for other child support orders (from previous divorces, if any). In some states, child support ends at eighteen; in others it can continue (for instance if a child is a full-time student principally dependent on a parent) until the age of twenty-two or twenty-three. Oftentimes, both parents will feel that there is a lack of money. The payee worries that there's not enough; the payor can't imagine how he or she will survive paying.

Unlike asset and debt distribution, which tend to be final after a divorce, a change in circumstances post-divorce may affect the terms of the flow of money between your households even after your agreement is signed. This includes circumstances such as unanticipated needs of the child, including braces, hearing aids, and other medical needs; costly extracurricular activities for your child; a new job, the loss of a job, or a nonworking parent entering or re-entering the workforce.

Your priority right now is to research the child support laws in your state. Take time to learn the formula(s) used by your state court to determine the amount deemed suitable for payment, and see where you fit in. When it was time for Elena to sort out the terms of her divorce, her thoughts on the aspect of money were fairly revolutionary and an empowering example for others in her position. Her example of asking for what's needed and then taking responsibility for her circumstances might surprise and inspire you.

When I was presented with the question of child support, I chose to ask for the minimal amount. Why? The fear in the pit of my stomach at that moment was my wake-up call. I realized I hadn't really taken responsibility for my financial health, and this was my moment. I gave myself an assignment to start caring about my own capacity to earn money and thrive financially. I began checking my balances daily, paying attention to my credit card spending, and considering alternate streams of revenue. If this resonates with you, take time to learn, earn, and save as much as you can for your financial well-being. A dear teacher of mine reminds me that every time I set one dollar aside for savings or investments, I'm paying my future self.

To be clear, I'm not suggesting you live beneath your current circumstances. I'm recommending that you ask for what you'll need—and not more—to care well for your children and yourself. When you are reasonable and graceful around money, money will be reasonably and gracefully returned to you. Money is really just energy, and whatever you put out there will come back. Here is a short meditation to remember the steady presence of abundance in your life, and to move forward gracefully without grasping.

Meditation to Remember the Presence of Abundance

Begin in a comfortable seat, on a chair or the floor. Start by creating an equal inhale and exhale, breathing in through your nose into your belly for three counts, and exhaling from your belly out your nose for three counts. Then increase to four counts in, four counts out. Then to five, then six if you can, all the way to eight counts in, eight counts out. By the time you reach eight counts, you'll feel more connected to a sensation of fullness within and around you.

Now that you've established that steady, even breathing pattern, begin to clean your internal slate. See the slate as a blackboard being erased, creating an empty space for something new to be written on it.

In your mind, one at a time, draw little images of the material possessions of your marriage, starting with the least meaningful to the most meaningful. Do you have the courage to hold the eraser yourself, and be willing to let those things go, one at a time, to feel who you are without them?

You're becoming clearer, more ready to receive, more capable of growth and learning. You're ready to let go of the old reminders that tether you and your family to the past. This is when you move from the past-present to the future-present, and actually design your own willingness to step into the freshness of the future. Your practice of steady breathing helps you be aware as the signs of your future present themselves to you.

Alimony in the Twenty-First Century

Divorce is a financially intimidating idea, even with current laws that are explicitly designed to protect both parties, especially if your marriage was comprised of only one income. In most states, there is still the concept of alimony, also known as spousal support or spousal maintenance. The general idea of such support dates back to biblical times or earlier, when it was declared that "a man must provide sustenance to a woman who has borne him children."

Throughout much of history, the man was the financial provider, with the woman in the role of the homemaker and caretaker. The landscape shifted in the late 1970s, when the U.S. Supreme Court ruled against gender bias in alimony awards. Interestingly, even today when wives often outearn their husbands in certain areas of the country, few men are actually receiving alimony. When I last looked at the statistics, fewer than 4 percent of alimony awards were granted to men. This may be because they take an uneven distribution of other property, or because they waive their right to it more swiftly than women. Why? Perhaps due to gender normative expectations, or because men continue to have more earning power outside the home.

How does paying or accepting alimony feel? Are you struggling with guilt over accepting money from your ex, or are you okay with it? Maybe you don't want to be a burden, but you cannot support yourself and your child(ren) either. My first suggestion is always the same. Forgive yourself, then figure out how to become self-sufficient so you needn't accept payment for too long. After Elena became financially independent, she told her ex that she'd like her financial support rerouted to their son's college fund. She made that possible for herself, and serves as an example for her friends and colleagues going through divorce.

And if you find yourself grappling with the apparent inequity of supporting a spouse, you aren't alone—this issue is complicated. Supporting a former spouse, especially if you don't have children or if child support is already being paid, can bring about resentment. Often the original reason people choose to separate relates to whether a stay-at-home spouse should return to work. Then, ironically, in divorce, the provider spouse may be ordered to continue to support this underemployed partner for years to come. If this is your case, you're not alone either. Review the chapters on clarity and peace, and take care of your inner state.

In certain cases, alimony may depend solely on spending habits or earning ability. It may be impacted by a variety of factors, such as the length of the marriage, the health and age of each party, the likelihood of future inheritance, vocational skills, education, earning potential (actual earning potential versus imagined potential), or circumstances causing you (or your spouse) to forfeit the ability to save or earn money in anticipation of future earnings or inheritance(s).

Alimony laws vary drastically from state to state, so ask your lawyer and learn the laws. In some places, alimony is not recognized at all. Some areas honor alimony as something that goes on forever until the former spouse either remarries or dies. Other jurisdictions limit the number of years and/or the amount of money someone may collect as alimony. Some states stipulate that the marriage is required to last for a specific term of years for alimony to even be considered. Whether you feel you've been slighted or shortchanged by the order of the court, your work is to create peace within yourself and maintain that quality of softness no matter what your thinking mind presents as a reason for anger. Elena offers a one-minute meditation inspired by Thich Nhat Hanh's book *Anger* for that moment of reckoning when it seems you'd have every right to be angry, but can turn to your practice to transform it. Take this moment to breathe three deep breaths. Then repeat this paragraph aloud or to yourself.

I am learning how to take good care of my anger, and in doing so, I'm taking better care of myself. Anger hurts my heart and blocks me from true love. I set myself free from this anger right now. I breathe [*take a deep breath*] and I am softer. I am doing my best, right this moment. I am setting myself free. I am setting myself FREE.

CHAPTER 9

Parenting Forward

———

The Legacy You Will Leave

Your ex is not your child's ex.
—DK SIMONEAU, CHILDREN'S BOOK AUTHOR

Your children's success after you separate or divorce depends on whether you manage to keep communication open and relationships clear. Separation need not trigger passive, pervasive anxiety. Instead, make it your mission to improve all the relationships in your home consciously and with care. You're now creating a healthier life for your children apart from your ex than you ever were able to provide for them together. While it's best if both of you establish good relations with your kids as a united front, even if your ex isn't able or willing to create a harmonious co-parenting plan, you can still cultivate conscious, positive relationships with each of your kids, to their great benefit.

Marriage doesn't necessarily foster a child's well-being. What does matter for the child's future mental and physical health is a loving relationship with at least one parent, who provides stability, structure, and a safe space in which to grow.

While divorce affects most children in the short term, if both the separating parents demonstrate care and love, coupled with respect, clarity, and consistency, the children of divorce grow up to be resilient, sensitive, strong members of society. As you read and learn about your options regarding parenting plans, keep your mind and heart open. To grow up as secure, confident adults, your children need to be raised in a stable, loving, emotionally nourishing environment. Please underline, highlight, and remember this: married or divorced, children are most damaged when they perceive or experience high levels of conflict between the parents.

Rather than focusing on the disappointment of your divorce, consider the situation from your child's vantage point. Happier, well-adjusted parents will lead them through life knowing they are loved and cared for by both parents, who respect each other even though they're no longer together.

By mitigating conflict and maximizing quality time with your children when they are with you, you'll create a nurturing two-household childhood for them—possibly even better than it would have been if you'd stayed together. Back in the early eighties, when my parents separated and later divorced, they chose what was then considered to be an avant-garde custody arrangement. My dad moved around the corner from our family home in Brooklyn, and my brother and I switched households every other day, alternating our weekends with each parent. Currently, shared parenting arrangements are relatively commonplace.

Some claim that such arrangements are too chaotic. I firmly believe that contempt and conflict, both overt and implicit, are what interfere with your child's stable development, not the number of transitions between households. Today, while there is a strong trend in the direction of sharing parenting rights and responsibilities, there is not one usual or normal plan. Here we explore how to curate the best plan for you family.

With regard to your parenting plan, design an arrangement that prioritizes the physical and emotional needs of your children. When possible, always put them first. Let's explore parenting through the lenses of patience, respect, clarity, peace, and forgiveness.

Patience

In an ideal world, you and your ex will try to maintain continuity and consistency of rules and expectations between your homes, but over time, your two households will likely become more different than alike. Particularly after your children have had a chunk of time at your ex's home, they may behave in new and unexpected ways. Remember, your kids are managing divergent expectations in each house, and it's your task to practice patience with them as they navigate two homes. It's also your task to be patient with your ex, with your ex's significant other, and especially with yourself when potentially chaotic situations arise. Patience affords you the pause in which to consider all angles. Patience also grants you the presence to respond only after you have calmed down. And when you disagree with the other parent's style or decisions, please speak about it during a time when you're not heated, and definitely not in front of the kids. Practice being patient enough to note what needs to be addressed later, in a quiet, calm space, when you both have a chance to decompress and settle. Patience is like a muscle you're developing, and practice makes perfect.

Respect

Your children's sense of who they are depends almost entirely on how you and your co-parent respect each other. Please be mindful of what you say about their other parent, because children and teens integrate what they hear into who they are. Negative words and actions directed to or about their other parent are destructive to children. Model respect by demonstrating it to your ex and any extended family members who enter into your children's world. Even when you are not feeling full of respect for them, you can be respectful of the situation and of their role as your child's parent. Stay calm and collected in the face of challenging interactions.

Ask for—don't demand—accommodations in your parenting plan when these are necessary. If you are respectful of others, you're more likely to be treated the same way in return. Respect also means not saying what you might be thinking in front of the kids—for example, saying your child's stepmother is limited, unattractive, and/or boring. If there are any real concerns over other members of a blended family—a stepsister appears to have a bad influence on your daughter, for example—take it up with your ex gracefully, not in the presence of your children. If you can't resolve a serious problem to your mutual satisfaction, then it may be time to engage a parenting coordinator, your lawyer, or a mediator to begin to move forward. If necessary, revisit your lawyer and appear before a judge about changing your parenting plan.

Clarity

Your clearheaded assessment of your family's needs is essential in creating a parenting plan. Considering the factors described below, create a well-structured flow for the children. Once you have this set, you can begin to be flexible with each other and with your children. Most children will have feelings and thoughts about and reactions to the custody arrangement. Support your kids through this transition by validating their feelings and giving them ample space to process. Consider taking them to a therapist who specializes in working with children whose family is in transition. Create clarity with regard to the parenting plan by sharing the details of the schedule with your kids. Take the time to listen to what your children need, and pay attention to what your ex says they need. Always keep space open for your ex and your children to say more, by asking in the moment if there is more to say, more to discuss. By listening to them in an attentive, caring way, you're creating a template for them to do the same for you.

Peace

Fashion a parenting plan that prioritizes peace, one that minimizes the potential for conflict in the future. Focus on your child's best interests instead of your own needs and desires. As you'll see in a few years, when you meet the needs of your kids, they'll grow up well-adjusted and secure, which will help your family overall. Prioritize peace in your negotiations by verbally marking when you and your ex agree: "I've just noticed we're in agreement on that!" Your calm, peaceful resonance will open the door to kindness throughout the process. By maintaining this priority in your mind and heart, even when matters are less than peaceful, you'll make things easier.

Forgiveness

Forgive yourself for having a hard time. Forgive yourself for not wanting to share your children. Forgive yourself for not giving your children the nuclear family you had imagined. Forgive yourself for having to go to work and put your kids in child care. Forgive your ex as he/she struggles with time management. Forgive your ex's mother, who has a temper that you're now seeing in your child. Forgive your own mother (or anyone else) when she can't stop lamenting your failure. And if you're thinking now about your own family's version of these examples, be sure to revisit your parenting plan to minimize conflict and facilitate forgiveness going forward. When you forgive, you open your heart to true, abiding compassion. Elena has a story to share that might serve as inspiration as you rewrite your own.

Parents Divided, Family United

Elena's experience speaks volumes about her commitment to keeping her family united even after a slightly rocky start to her divorce. Even if your divorce has begun in a contentious fashion—in fact, even if one or both of you have behaved disgracefully thus far—your vision *matters*. If you have a partner who has acted up and you're the one who's owed an apology, it's still your highest, finest work to make space for a future as a functional, transformed family. Five years from now when you look back on this time, you'll remember the poise you brought to this demanding, tumultuous moment.

Elena had the focused intention to create a calm, stable context for her son, including a clear structure with love as the imperative. She's managed to shift the dynamic in her family by holding on to this vision and displaying equanimity.

When I began deconstructing my marriage, I received compelling coaching on how to design a co-parenting relationship that would make all of us proud. At that time, I was struggling with addiction, general malaise, and a marked lack of focus that kept me fearful and emotionally stagnant. Underlying it all, while I understood that I could solve this by changing my own behavior, I still wasn't clear on my own personal power to heal the situation. I wasn't practicing compassion for myself; I was practicing self-sabotage, then blaming the rest of the world for my problems.

First, thanks to the coaching, I began telling the truth from moment to moment, both to myself and to those around me. I saw the human condition so clearly—how often we lie and fabricate reality. So I owned my part and apologized for my contribution to the demise of our marriage and my unhealthy behaviors. In choosing radical honesty, I learned first how to approach myself with kindness, then began showing more decency and humanity in my interactions with my ex. It took time, but he felt the shift and began trusting me more.

That helped us design our future apart, with a conscious focus on handling things skillfully and intelligently. Now, eight years later, he and I have developed a true friendship. And when one of us falters or forgets, the other holds the elegance for both of us. With our son, we are both committed to staying positive, supportive, and kind, in order to build a solid foundation for his sense of self. Especially poignant for me is how our son is palpably comforted when his dad and I simply stand close to each other and smile at him, even during the toughest times. And his happiness in those fleeting moments is enough to inspire us to continue to work on being closer and relatively happy.

The Meaning of Custody:
Legal and Physical Custody

There are two types of custody: legal and physical. Legal custody gives you decision-making authority over your children. Physical custody refers to where your children live. You and your ex may be able to have joint physical custody, in which your children have two legal addresses. In some places, this is the new norm. It's also possible to have sole physical custody yet share legal custody, which means your child lives with you but you continue to make decisions (primarily concerning health, education, and religion) together. Some jurisdictions even allow legal custody around certain "spheres of custody." This means that while the parties generally share legal custody one parent gets final decision-making power for certain issues such as medical issues. Many couples who don't get along are still able to effectively share legal custody of their children, because they do agree on matters relating to the health, education, and religion of their children. Note that throughout this conversation I will use the words *custody* and *parenting* interchangeably.

Financially, in many jurisdictions today, the amount of child support will vary significantly depending on the physical parenting or custody plan. From a legal perspective, the parents' financial considerations should never enter the conversation about custody. Practically speaking, however, be sure that you understand the interplay between custody and child support in your jurisdiction. This full understanding will help your family avoid conflict later on regarding the financial responsibilities of each parent as it relates to matters of custody. Ask lots of questions of your attorney on this matter so you can be informed.

Creating Your Perfect Custody/ Parenting Plan: Eight Considerations

Before you even begin to formulate a parenting plan, here are eight important points to take into consideration.

1. There is no perfect parenting plan.

In addition to being a divorce lawyer and a divorce mediator, I also act as a neutral third-party parenting plan coordinator in cases where conflict cannot be resolved. Don't sacrifice "good enough" waiting for "perfect." No parenting plan is going to be perfect. Compromise is needed, and both parents should be prepared to display maturity and give a little in the design of the plan. Take a deep breath and a step back, and try not to obsess about creating the perfect plan. Focus on what your entire family needs to feel comfortable, and do your best to behave with kindness and compassion.

2. Listen to the professionals, but trust your intuition.

Refining your intuition is key here, and practices such as journaling, movement, meditation, and even prayer can help you figure out what is true for you. Practice trusting your inner voice. Be cautious about collecting advice from those other than those closest to you and your lawyer; it serves only to plant self-doubt in your head. Many people will offer their opinions as to what "works best for you." Though they may be well-intentioned, it's impossible for others to know the range and nuance of your family's immediate and future needs. Also, beware when comparing your situation to that of anyone else. While there may be obvious similarities between your circumstances, remember no two pictures are the same. Your attorney can help you suss out what's needed and what's possible, and listening to your own heart's deeper message can help you create the conditions for the ideal to emerge.

3. Create a plan based on today, not tomorrow.

Make choices based upon the present circumstances with an eye to the future, but don't get too caught up in the what-ifs. As you craft your co-parenting agreement, be aware that parenting plans can be changed. Unlike property distribution, which is usually final, anything pertaining to children is likely open to a legal revisit, months and even years into the future. Focus on your present circumstances and the needs of your children and what you are certain about in the future. For instance, if your children are small now but will be going to kindergarten in the future, that is a foreseeable circumstance that you can write into the agreement today. However, do not get bogged down worrying over unknowable future circumstances.

4. Make sure the plan is specific and predictable.

Set yourselves up for success by addressing the specifics when you first create your parenting plan. Some families are able to function without a detailed structure, but in my experience, a clear plan minimizes questions and complications. The more specific the plan is, the less room there is for conflict. A plan that is exhaustively thorough makes everyone's lives easier with regard to scheduling and facilitates enforcement by a court in case anything goes awry (which ideally it won't). You can always refine your family's arrangement as needs and schedules shift and when emergencies arise.

5. Be clear on one set of rules and boundaries for both households.

Kids need boundaries and rules in order to thrive; these are a crucial aspect of healthy childhood development. Make it a priority to design your family's behavioral expectations, and then collectively enforce them. No matter what type of parenting plan you devise, this is paramount. Undermining your ex by being more lenient and permissive than the rules allow only hurts your children in the long run. And it is not going to make your children love you more; it's only going to serve as a model for future bad behavior.

As I mentioned earlier, when I grew up, my parents had family meetings several times a year. These involved me, my brother, my two parents, and sometimes even their significant others. At these meetings, everyone openly discussed parenting policies and rules; thus it was made clear that, although our parents were divorced, we children were not in charge. Again, while I found these meetings unpleasant and mildly irritating, especially during my teen years, in retrospect I recognize the gift my parents gave us in creating this safe space for clear communication and well-defined parameters.

Rules and boundaries will vary from family to family depending on the age of your kids, family and individual interests, and special needs. Plan accordingly. Do your best to be on the same page with one another. Here is a list for you to begin crafting your boundaries as a family—apart, but still a family. This way you can be on the same team, with the same expectations, together.

- Bedtime

Homework

Allowances

Clothing choices

Curfews

Screen time and other media use

Driving

Extracurricular activities

Social activities

6. Consider the distance between your homes.

Sharing equal custody with multiple transitions weekly works best for families when both parents live close to each other, preferably in the same school district. A few points to consider: How much time will your children have to spend in a car each week to get back and forth between homes? Would a longer block of time in each place (trading off each week instead of every day or every few days) make scheduling easier? In my case, my parents lived so close to each other that I could just walk down the street and visit with the other parent, which made transitions easy. Even when the households are widely separated, a shared parenting plan may work. Even with one parent in California and the other in Maine, the kids can live with one parent for the school year and the other during breaks and summer vacations. Clarity and flexibility is key.

7. Take everyone's personalities into account with regard to daily planning.

Know your strengths and weaknesses, as individuals and as a family. Especially if your plan involves multiple children and frequent transitions, ideally you will both be strong planners and communicators. Ensure your family's success with a weekly list of tasks and responsibilities, even using an online family calendar for easy reminders. Some kids and parents keep track of belongings and schedules more naturally than others. When activities and schedules vary from week to week, there is greater potential to misplace soccer cleats, forget ballet slippers, and lose homework. Even if you consider yourself to be a perfect planner and communicator, consider a parenting plan with precision and predictability. Thankfully, there are many accessible, efficient co-parenting tools available online to help you and your ex co-parent in your post-separation journey. Simple tools like an online scheduling platform such as Google Calendar can help streamline complicated scheduling; each of you has a color and it's easy to see who is where and when.

Our Family Wizard is an ever-evolving tool that can be viewed and shared with your professionals as well as your family, in order to keep everyone up-to-date on all sorts of communications including schedules, and even finances. There are also educational and motivational sites designed to help you navigate your parenting such as UpToParents.org. Your attorney, your mediator, or your local area court will likely have the most updated, relevant resources.

8. Consider the reality of your schedules and commitments.

While a shared parenting plan may sound wonderful in theory, it may be impossible in practice. If this is the way you want to go, your schedule and your commitments must allow for it. Perhaps you travel extensively for work, or you put in long hours during the week. Perhaps you like to go out often socially, or perhaps there's a safety issue in your ex's home. Please don't sign an agreement that obligates you to be parenting when you aren't available, or one that compromises the child's emotional or physical safety, or even one in which your parenting will interfere with your preferred lifestyle. Even if the idea is hard to swallow, giving up custody in exchange for visitation rights would most likely be in the best interest of your entire family. Regardless of the parenting plan you reach, make sure to be specific about the following:

Vacations

Holidays

Birthdays

Parent-teacher meetings

Drop-offs and pickups at school and events

Elena's story is a good example of a separating couple who are both committed to the concept of being better apart.

I felt most vulnerable sitting at the table in the conference room with attorneys, at least until I chose to turn my feeling of powerlessness into total empowerment. That was the moment I chose to settle into myself, speak with confidence, and stay humble. I chose to leave behind fighting and fear and cultivate care and emotional consistency.

From the start, our parenting plan was to communicate clearly with each other in order to optimize the situation and allow for everyone's schedules. Yes, at times one of us would act selfishly and make things difficult. We excelled in apologizing when we were wrong. We'd own our part, discuss our missteps, and do it over (literally, say it over or do it over); we'd talk about how we would have handled things differently. Those moments helped our son see fallibility, ownership, and responsibility in action. As a result, we're now experiencing his readiness to apologize and own his part in his interactions and relations.

The particulars were pretty simple. Our family has a relatively set schedule, with certain days at Dad's and certain days with me. That structure has always worked, and even when Jonah's dad needs more flexibility, we can easily adjust our arrangement to best meet our family's present needs.

While I've always felt lucky to have this easeful arrangement, it's really a result of many small actions we've all taken, including compromises and kindnesses.

Custody or Parenting Plan Alternatives

Traditionally in the United States, kids from most divorced households in the past several decades lived with their mother and had weekend visitations with their father. Just take a peek at an old episode of *Mad Men* if you want to get a picture of what a typical custody plan looked like circa 1962. The father was typically the provider working outside the home, and the mother was at home tending to the children. Dad swooped in on Friday night or Saturday morning and took the kids back to his place for the weekend. Maybe he had them for an evening midweek, too. The ex-wife got a full-time or part-time job, if needed (and most did), ran the family household, and kept up as best she could with the help of child support and possibly, if she was lucky enough to live in a state that allowed it, alimony.

As women increasingly entered the workplace, the landscape of child custody started to shift. Initially, women still were assumed to be the caregivers and thus were most often granted custody. By the 1980s, however, fathers started to become more vocal about having more time with their kids. As men got more involved with child rearing and household duties, fathers now requested more, if not equal, time with their children. Today, it's quite typical in many parts of the country to see kids sharing their time fairly equally between the households of their two parents.

Shared Custody:
The New Face of Co-Parenting

In an ideal shared custody arrangement, children have two primary homes and move easily between them, with each home feeling like theirs. Proponents of this style of parenting feel it's good for their children, as it allows them to develop strong, safe bonds with each parent. In this situation, parents can choose designated times and days in which they will be more available physically, emotionally, and energetically. Shared custody works only if each parent is willing and able to be fully available to their children when it's their time to be the designated provider. My father often spoke of quality over quantity when it came to our time together; he was mindful about being fully engaged with my brother and me during our times together.

If you and your spouse can agree to work cooperatively, shared custody can be a wonderful way to parent forward. Even if you're arguing over other issues, shared custody arrangements are often still workable. Be sure to create a firm foundation for your children by crafting clear expectations in each household to minimize chaos and conflict. Your children will thrive with the two of you working together, using one set of boundaries and rules between the two homes.

Be aware of your language as you refer to your children's time with you. To your child it is just time, rather than Mom's time or Dad's time. Don't give them the smaller room because they're with you only part-time; with shared parenting, a child is only anywhere part-time, which can be taxing for children emotionally. Remember, your two houses are your child's one home. Shared parenting can be arranged in any variety of ways. Here are a few possible options.

Alternate each week with one parent.

Alternate Monday and Tuesday with one parent, Wednesday and Thursday with the other, and alternating weekends.

Alternate every day and weekends (like I did).

Spend the school year with one parent and summer and vacation time with the other (in case of very long distances between the parents).

If you can visualize your plan and you're both on the same page, then you can really make any parenting plan work. If both parents live close to each other, it can be very nourishing for the children to see both parents as often as they can. If you're concerned about potential conflict in the transitions from one home to the other, consider doing the majority of transitions during drop-off and pickup from school, so you two parents can coexist without having to see each other, which is easiest for some families.

Sole Custody:
The Traditional Solution

While a shared parenting plan is an attractive and feasible construct for many families, it may not be for you. The other viable option is the traditional sole custody plan. This kind of setup worked just fine for decades, and continues to function well for many families today. Many divorcing parents who get along quite well employ this arrangement because it's more comfortable for their family. Some couples find that their kids love being in both homes.

In families where one spouse works long hours, travels much of the time, or is an alcoholic or substance abuser, sole custody is the only option. Similarly, if one parent is unavailable or undependable, emotionally or physically abusive, or unfit in some other way, sole custody is optimal. These are the types of situations that often land in the hands of a judge to make the ruling, so be forewarned that you'll need the help of a lawyer and perhaps other professionals for guidance.

Nesting:
An Alternative Way to Co-Parent

In some families, instead of children splitting time between two homes, the children remain in the family home and the parents alternate moving in and out. In such cases, the parents are essentially supporting three households (or share two, but that's much more rare). Typically nesting offers a short-term solution in a trial separation, early in the divorce, or when the children are almost out of high school and the arrangement is going to be short-term by design. Even in the short term, a clear set of boundaries within a well-crafted parenting plan is essential in order to keep conflict to a minimum.

In a nesting scenario, the parents live out of a suitcase rather than the children. As a result, some view this as the most child-centric arrangement. Proponents of nesting like the idea because it creates less disruption for the kids. On the other hand, some say that this arrangement potentially underscores the emotional and logistical troubles that already exist in your family. For example, if you value neatness and your ex doesn't, you'll still be living with that mess in your shared nest. Still others view nesting as a Band-Aid solution delaying the inevitable long-term solution of a plan allowing for the children to seamlessly flow between the parents.

If you choose to nest, you'll want to design clear boundaries around socializing with your new significant other(s) in the children's residence. Here are some considerations to keep in mind regarding nesting:

Late-night stays with new relationships—how soon and how often?

Sleepovers with new relationships—how soon and how often?

What personal items of the parents remain in the family home?

Who stocks the fridge? Is it one of you or will you alternate?

Who cleans the house and/or pays the housecleaner?

Designing Your Parenting Plan

Once you and your spouse have agreed in theory to the outline of your parenting plan, it's time to outline the details. Avoid future conflict by having the difficult conversations about particulars early in your divorce process; this helps keep the peace for your entire family. If currently you have primary parenting time and you're reluctant to set a schedule including the other parent, please know this: including your co-parent may actually make your life easier in the long run. The other party then has a set schedule, and you need not be burdened by your co-parent's annoying you. Once a clear parenting plan is in place, your family dynamic may begin to settle and you each will be free to enjoy the time you spend with your kids.

When designing your plan, include all reasonable details, such as who gets the child(ren) when you have an emergency or during holidays and days off from school. As tedious as it may be, anticipate the seemingly minute issues in advance and take the time to find the points of compromise. An agreement with open-ended language such as "open and reasonable parenting time" is not actually an agreement; it's merely an agreement to agree. Be aware that agreements to agree carry no weight in court—meaning that if you go to court complaining about your ex's wishy-washy summer vacation schedule, the judge gets to make decisions on behalf of your kids. Get specific now in order to avoid arguments later.

Difficult Ex? How to Nurture Happy Kids Anyway

Even if you think your ex is undependable or difficult to work with, remember that your children have an instinctive bond to their parents, both of them. Even in cases where children are utterly disappointed in their relationship with a parent, that parent still fundamentally comprises half of who they are. Encourage the flow of communication and love between child and parent. And if they have a particularly disappointing other parent, be sure they know that you'll be there for them, and while you will listen to the child, you will not be speaking ill of their other parent. Your mission is to stay positive, with boundaries, and envision the other parent doing the best he or she can do. Even if that vision isn't necessarily true, your forgiving mindset will create a compassionate environment for all.

The Role of a Parenting Coordinator

When there is an unresolved dispute over a parenting plan, some states have professionals available to serve as parenting coordinators. A parenting coordinator may have decision-making authority or may serve simply in a role similar to that of a directive mediator, only with a narrower focus on parenting issues. This person may be privately compensated or state paid, and would typically be a mental health professional or an attorney who's been trained specifically for this role.

If you live in one of the states where parenting coordinators are not court ordered, you may consider finding and hiring one to help you move your case (your life) forward more quickly and with less expense than a trial. But be aware. Depending on where you live and what kind of agreement you sign, your parenting coordinator may have the authority to create binding decisions much like a judge, without necessarily having any significant experience or training. After understanding the needs and dynamic of your family during a series of meetings, talks, or interviews, your parenting coordinator may make recommendations regarding important issues such as health care, school selection, schedule changes, and vacations. Using a parenting coordinator to determine custody works well in two situations: when both parties are willing to work toward a viable resolution and when you have a difficult ex. In the latter case, your parenting coordinator may be well suited to negotiate smaller parenting issues. Consult your local counsel to see how parenting coordinators are utilized where you live.

Parenting Empowerment Writing Exercise

If you took for granted all your time with your children and now find yourself wanting to engage more consciously during your quality time with them, this simple exercise will start your creative juices flowing and will help you to rebuild your confidence about your ability to parent and stay connected to your children. Both are simply a matter of practice.

If you feel that there is distance between you and your child(ren) and don't quite know how to bridge that gap, or if you simply wish to create more meaning in your interactions, make a list of all the specific activities you've done with your child(ren). If you have more than one, you can make a separate list for each child, or one of the two together.

Visualize each activity; see it in your mind. But even more importantly, feel your connection in each moment. Each time you do this, you're reminding yourself of the sensation of that bond and neurologically evoking that closeness.

Make another list of the current connection times you have with your child(ren), taking into account your work schedule and their school and activities schedules. This doesn't have to be an extensive list of outings; just note the moments of being together, even if it's a weekly car ride. To become more consciously aware of your times together is valuable to both of you and will help you enjoy that time with more care and creativity.

Create a list or vision board of how you ideally see yourself spending those moments of time. This will serve as your invitation to bring your ideal times with them to fruition.

Finally, devise an action plan to put these ideas into action. It could be as simple as spending five minutes a day simply listening to your child(ren). Maybe just watching a movie or eating a meal together without distraction. Any action you can take to help them feel heard and supported by you will help you all move forward in a positive way.

Elena recommends a few words you can use to remind yourself of your intention when it comes to your parenting, particularly in moments of conflict: "I nourish my connection to my family with my listening, my learning, and my love."

CHAPTER 10

Really, We're Better Apart

———

Separation has real consequences, and at this moment you might not be sure whether this is the best option for you. As I noted in the Pause prior to chapter 1, after some reflection you and your partner may ultimately decide that you may become better together. But, if separating is the answer for you and your family, as painful and exhausting as it may be in the moment, please know that shedding your difficult, ambivalent, dysfunctional, or painful relationship may release you for a brighter, better future. Regardless of your circumstances, as you two move through a productive and compassionate separation, you'll emerge ready to receive new love and adventures.

If you practice treating yourself and your family with kindness throughout your process, you may find that you and your former spouse are much better friends or co-parents than you were lovers or partners. Some people are able to do this almost without thinking. Others have to pay close attention at every step along the way. For most, there are hard days and easy days. There are times you may wonder why you couldn't make it work, and times you may rejoice that you've parted ways.

Mastering the practices of patience, respect, clarity, peace, and forgiveness, you'll advance elegantly through your separation or divorce, particularly if children are involved. Be gentle with yourself as you forge through this uncharted territory. Maybe your own parents have modeled a graceful process for you. Perhaps your family has endured a hostile, fractious divorce. Regardless of the circumstances in your family of origin, when you remember to listen, slow down, and engage in the practices explored throughout this book, you will see results for your entire tribe. Let's take a peek at dating during divorce and at some of the common twists and turns of the divorce and post-divorce territory.

Dating and Friendship

Affairs during marriage are staggeringly common, as is dating during divorce. No matter how strong your impulse is to be honest with your ex, maintain your privacy with regard to your personal life until the papers are signed and the ink is dry. Why? While you may be madly in love with someone else, your post-divorce relationship with your ex needs to be treated with the same five tenets we've discussed in this book: patience, respect, clarity, peace, and even forgiveness, especially when integrating your new relationship into your children's lives.

You'll create a more favorable outcome for all by keeping your relationship quiet and private until all is resolved. Even if your ex is the one who'd initiated divorce, most humans find it hard to see an ex's new relationships flourish. Grab your pen and underline the following two rules.

Even when the divorce is fresh, do your best to refrain from posting on social media about your new relationship, and ask that your new paramour do the same. Don't lie about your status, but do protect the dignity of your former spouse, your children, and yourself. How? Be discreet, no flaunting.

Prioritize your kids. Keep your private relations respectful and quiet.

In my experience, clients often fall blindly in love with new mates and then immediately introduce them to the children, a practice with which I strongly disagree. Respect your children's need to re-calibrate and readjust, and first establish your new relationship with your children. This does not mean you can never integrate your new partner into your family—it just means you should give it some time. Maybe even just six months after you have established sepa-rate households before bringing a new love interest into your chil-dren's already complicated life. You may enjoy the company of your paramour when your children are with your co-parent. If you have your children all the time, be sure to set aside certain days where you are focused on your children, giving them meaningful quality time. Granting your kids this time to acquaint themselves with their new life is crucial to their confidence later on. Be patient.

Early in my law career, I was impatient and wished my cases would be resolved more quickly; as I mentioned earlier, "divorce is like a fine wine—it needs time to age." While you may be further along in your emotional healing than your ex or your family, it's im-portant to give everyone their time to process. Slowest is quickest.

Blended Families

In today's post-divorce world, blended, hybridized new families are a reality. Such integration requires that you find the deepest compassion. Becoming a stepparent or welcoming a stepparent into your life (whether your ex's new partner or yours) might be the most complicated transition in the entire divorce, but it can also be incredibly rewarding.

In certain circumstances, you'll find you have an ally in your ex's new partner. For your children, witnessing your healthy relations with their stepparent(s) is a clear opportunity to watch emotional intelligence in action. Integration takes time and patience. Recognize that it can be difficult, and practice making it easy. In creating a new conscious family, enter each exchange with respect and love. Prioritize consistent quality time with each child, remembering that their perspective on this blended family can be vastly different from yours. Ask questions, offer your assistance and presence, let go of your expectations, and be of loving service.

Here is a glimpse into the potential complexities of blending families to provide you with some insight into what can happen:

A difficult ex on the other side complains that you're overstepping boundaries or acting too much like a friend.

Your new beloved has a child who's highly protective of his biological parent. "You're not my mother." You have responsibility, yet without authority.

You may be expected to do all your new stepchildren's homework with them, but you're not permitted to attend parent-teacher conferences or special meetings about their learning.

Your biological child(ren) clash with the children of your new partner.

Your new partner's ex gives their child a large allowance or a device that you do not condone for your own kids, and your children resent it.

First, recognize that this is hard for everyone. Assume each party is doing the best he or she can. There is no script for this process, so bring love to it. Expanding your compassion is the only way to peace.

Your ex's new partner can actually be your greatest ally if you engage in a meaningful way that supports what you both need. Observe the dynamics of the situation. If you feel comfortable doing it, Elena recommends asking lots of questions, being of service, and not imposing your own needs too quickly. For instance, perhaps your ex is not great at keeping a schedule or is notoriously late. You may notice that these "habits of being" change when they pair up with someone who favors organization, and your ex's new partner actually helps you get your interactions (and parenting plan or payments) on track.

With four parents, multiple children, different rules, and varying expectations, chaos can ensue. How to mitigate that? Elena offers three simple practices—inquiry, gratitude, and boundaries.

Inquiry

Ask questions first. How does this feel? How can I help? What feels best for you?

Gratitude

Thanking your family in advance of their completing what they're being asked to do helps move things forward in a pleasant and inspiring context.

Boundaries

If a situation becomes challenging, in a kind tone, offer to take the matter up at a later time and step away. Make it easy and safe to bring the topic up when things are less heated.

There's No Place Like Home

Your children must feel relatively at ease when in each home. Your job and privilege is to nourish your child's heart, mind, and soul by creating a calm, clean, safe space for him or her in which to grow and learn.

PRIORITY: If you perceive your child feels unsettled in the other parent's home, rather than criticizing that parent, send your child over with a favorite toy. Support your child by asking your ex how you can help if it seems like help is needed. In your own home, support your child in his or her activities and with homework. And remember, neither house should be all fun or all work. Ideally, your children have two stable, serene, supportive homes. And if this is not possible in both homes, do your part to make yours thus.

Again, your child's multiple residences collectively comprise his or her sense of home. Even if your resources or physical space are limited, and even if you're only a part-time parent, you must assist your children in creating a sense of ownership and pride in their physical environment within every home. If you're setting up a new room for your child, gather personal items or furniture that your child will find familiar and comforting. If new furniture is too expensive, consider allowing your child to select a new paint color for his or her room, or even for one wall of a room shared with a sibling or stepsibling.

If you're the parent who retains the family home, be especially mindful to refer to both residences, the other parent's and yours, as *home*. With a young child, explain that they'll now have two houses, and each is their home. With older kids, you can be more casual. Say "when you go home to Mom's" or "when you are at your home with Dad," and keep the tension out of your tone. Life is short, and your expressed permission for your children to feel relaxed and comfortable in the other parent's home is vital for their emotional well-being, their psychological and physical health.

If you're the parent about whom the child feels protective, remember that your child may be afraid to show kindness to the other parent if he or she perceives that you've been hurt or betrayed by that parent. While it may be affirming to have the children on your side, generously granting them the space to love and settle in with the other parent is optimal. And you'll notice that as the dust settles, your children will easily draw their own conclusions about your separation and create their own story based on your actions, not your words. Be strong, nurturing, and present. Ideally both of you will inspire each other to practice those qualities. Elena has a writing practice that can help you get clear on what you can do if your ex is making things difficult and contentious.

Morning Pages to Set the Tone for Your Day

This simple practice asks that you wake up and write about the tone or energy you wish to set for the day, which you'll all endeavor to maintain and uphold no matter what the external world brings. Take five or ten minutes and just write about what and how you'd like to be today. Communicate this to your kid(s) and let them in on your energetic reset each day. Watch what happens.

Holidays, Special Occasions, and Birthdays

Whether you are married or divorced, holidays and special occasions can be stressful. The societal and internal pressure to be upbeat and festive on such special days is significant, even if you are someone who's typically full of gusto and enthusiasm. Both Elena and I are clear on one practice here. Give yourself permission to feel. And if it's your turn for the holiday with your children, and your ex seems more equipped to hold the holiday cheer this year, consider allowing the children to spend time with your co-parent. Give your children the opportunity to witness your flexibility as you create positive choices based on current realities. The essence of holiday is celebration, so find a way for that to be optimized, whether with you or your co-parent.

Re-create your holiday so it suits you in your new life. Even if you're not quite up to it at first, take heart. With the passage of time, your sadness will subside and the spirits of all will lift. If you've never enjoyed the way holidays were handled during your relationship, reconfigure your holiday rituals. Acknowledge occasions in a manner that's meaningful to you.

How you create your child's experience around holidays and birthdays is likely to remain with them into adulthood. Model forgiveness and compassion. Some families are even able to share the festivities with ex-in-laws. It took time, but Elena and her ex choose to spend a number of occasions together each year, and have grown to value that time together. My family of origin has done the same for years. Some alternate holidays; others split them by the hour. Even if you would prefer not to, perhaps consider allowing your ex to have Christmas Eve each year if it's his family's special day; your generosity will be appreciated and the favor will be returned to you in years to come.

However you and your ex navigate the holidays, the greatest gift you can give your children is peace. If your child desires an extravagant gift and you cannot afford to give it on your own, consider giving a joint present. In doing so, you support each other and present your child with the example of a collaborative spirit, especially important for them to see during the separation and post-divorce. While blended families often have an initial period of unease or discomfort, in the child's world you're all family now. It can be incredibly healing to come together around important life events. If you're more financially fluid, consider giving your ex some extra money around the holiday toward a gift for your child. Create the spirit of giving.

When organizing your parenting or custody schedule around the holidays, give careful consideration not only to what your lawyer suggests (e.g., alternate school breaks on odd/even years) but also to how you design your intentional family rituals. If your ex's family has a big weekend away on every Memorial Day weekend, consider allowing your child to attend this every year. Opt to be magnanimous when you can; a small compromise on your side may feel tremendous to your ex. When your child is young, Halloween might be very important to both parents. Consider spending at least a short time together, even if just to allow both parents to see your small child dressed in his or her Halloween gear.

When it comes to birthdays, successfully separating families often alternate who hosts the birthday party each year. Some have two separate family celebrations (sounds excessive, but for some children it may mean extra fun and more gifts).

Creating New Rituals

Creating new rituals and traditions can be the most fulfilling practice of all. If it's your first holiday on your own, find some activities that lift your spirits. Join a friend's family, or if it suits you better, skip the fanfare and grant yourself a healing treatment—a pedicure, a visit to a spa, or even just a workout at your local gym. Take care of yourself. Set a new bar by putting your own needs first, especially during celebratory days, and actively nourishing yourself. The gift of solitude is precious, and you may find that when you begin treating yourself with care and love, the times you'll spend on your own will become treasured quiet moments in your life. Elena suggests taking a few moments to make a list of the potential holidays or occasions you'd be willing to spend solo in the coming weeks or months as a result of your separation.

First, create two columns on a piece of paper.

On the left, put holidays and occasions you're willing to give up for your kids to be with your ex and family. Be as specific as possible; none of this is set, and it's a way to acclimate yourself to be generous and even adventurous in your willingness to compromise.

On the right, list some of the ideal places and activities you'd like to visit or do during that solo time. Have you always wanted to go on a certain retreat? Perhaps you'd like to just spend some quiet time hiking in the woods or going to a museum with a dear friend. Is there an immersive weekend of art or music that you've put off your whole life? Have fun with both lists, and let them be works in progress. When emotions seem heightened, glance at these lists and remember that where there once was a perceived loss, there is now a chance to learn, grow, and nourish yourself.

Texting and Telephone Etiquette

With handheld devices and cell phones, it's easy to have direct communication with your child when they're with the other parent. You can text when convenient, and your child can reply when it suits the other family's needs. The only downside is that sometimes children text incessantly with the other parent when they're with you. If this describes your situation, speak to your ex about creating pockets of time in which to speak to your child, to have guaranteed quality time if that's desired.

If your ex enjoys using FaceTime with your children at bedtime, let them enjoy a few minutes of private time so that they can speak freely. The use of FaceTime can cause friction, particularly when you're on a luxurious vacation and your ex cannot afford such a trip. Be conscientious, be compassionate, and remember the Golden Rule: Do unto others as you would have them do unto you. It's important for your kids.

Last, work together with your ex to set aside time when all electronic devices are silenced for hours at a time, consistently in both homes. Science and common sense are reminding us that time away from electronics is crucial to your child's development.

Self-Care

Reminder of your new magic word: Self-Care. Take non-negotiable time out for yourself. Design and establish simple relaxation rituals to start your day. Before rising from bed, take five deep breaths in and out through your nose. When you take a shower, after you've rinsed, stand in the cleansing warm water for thirty seconds extra and continue to breathe. If time and money are limited, read a book, take a walk, or create a nourishing meal for yourself. Elena takes time every morning to spend time with herself, practicing a bit of yoga, breathing, perhaps writing, and meditation.

That time helps me set the tone for my day, seeing the compass points and gathering the energy for the day. Often that's when I am at my most creative. In talking to couples who are considering separation, I always encourage each person to set aside this morning time, earlier when they have the kid(s), so they can really feel like they have a moment with themselves. For me, that time in the morning makes all the difference in my capacity to respond positively to what comes over the course of a day.

Warning Signs That You Need a Refresher

Notice yourself snapping at your ex or your child? Take a step back to figure out what is troubling you. Once you've acknowledged what is causing your upset or reactivity, you can move forward productively, asking for what you need and delivering what others might require as well. Create a culture of care in your family using your practices of patience, respect, clarity, peace, and forgiveness.

And When Things Unexpectedly Change . . .

Perhaps you separated without a hitch, asset distribution and parenting plan sussed out effortlessly. Suddenly, months or years later, a new significant other or your own personal growth shifts the dynamic. Best practice: Return to the facts about what's essential for both sides, and explore where you are overreacting or seem to need a change. These five practices are daily cultivations, and your attention to them will yield results for your emotional life, your professional life, and most important, your family's life.

Acknowledgments

Better Apart began long before I'd considered becoming a divorce professional or a motivational *teacher*. I was raised in an incredibly nurturing environment by two strong-willed, independent, forward-thinking parents who prioritized my brother and me throughout the process of their divorce, which became the seed for my work.

My mother, Ruth, continues to be the model peacemaker, yet always holds her ground. My father, Peter, taught me to believe in myself and to advocate for those who couldn't stand up for themselves. My stepfather, Terry, thank you for always knowing when to take a step back. My brother, Marcello, thank you for being by my side, until my daily countdown for Cornell, to this day. To my four colorful grandparents, Walter and Ilse, German-Jewish Holocaust refugees in Riverdale, along with Joe (Guisseppe) and Sally (Salvatrice), in Brooklyn via Italy, thank you for loving and teaching me. And to my close extended family, my gratitude goes out to each of you for your presence and influence.

As a young attorney, I clerked for Justice Jeffrey Sunshine, currently the statewide coordinating judge for matrimonial cases. The experiences and insights afforded me by that position, working with the staff, clerks, court reporters, and court officers, contributed greatly to my depth of understanding regarding human relationship.

For all of the attorneys with whom I've worked closely during those years and beyond—especially Karen B. Soren and Aimee Richter—I'm forever grateful. For the last fourteen years, I've had the pleasure and honor to be in private practice with intelligent, capable colleagues and judges in Western Massachusetts that make our work rewarding even when it's grueling. And, of course, for each and every client who's engaged me to navigate the perilous divorce process, thank you for your trust.

Years ago, after more than a decade of frustration with the mechanistic approach to family law, I'd proclaimed to dear friends Atara Twersky, Dana Weiner, and my always-inspiring cousin Camilla Feibelman that the global transformation around relationships and divorce is just beginning. Shifting away from traditional litigation with the steady wisdom and support of these brilliant women, I've been committed to this important mission ever since. Thank you.

To my colleagues, friends, and relatives who've served as readers, inspirers, supporters, and confidants throughout this process, thank you for your friendship, patience, guidance, and energy. To name some, but certainly not all: Carol Park, Caryn Daniels, Joanne Wright, Cheryl Knopp, Liz Fischer, Emily Mines, Lynne Strasfeld, Jenny Yang, Robin Rudowitz, Trish Peterson, Amy Richter, Danielle DeMaio, Lisa Chin, Lisa Slow, Lauren Weinseir, Valerie Vignaux, Leslie Skantz, Elissa Miller, Jennifer Bracco, Trina Rondina, Beth Neumann, Lisa Kaufmann, Andrea DelDuca, Lisa Chin, Kim Lehrman, Pearl Lockwood, Lauren Weinseir, Renee Wetstein, Beth Notar, Caryn Brause, Amy Shatz, Wendy Foster, Jessica Berrien, Julie Jurman, the McGuires, and the Steinbergers.

And without Elena Brower, my inspiring friend and contributing author, readers of this book would miss an important dimension. Her steadfast commitment, clear purpose, and meticulously crafted contributions bring invaluable tools designed to enliven your practice and enrich your life. Elena is a force of nature—brilliant, hard-working, careful, but above all, caring. Her time and commitment to this project while managing her doTERRA business and her teaching commitments is appreciated more than she'll ever know.

Jen Marshall McVey, thank you for believing in the purpose and importance of this work. You have my eternal appreciation for helping me to skillfully communicate my vision early on.

Rousing gratitude to Karen Rinaldi, our editor extraordinaire, whose belief that relationships can and must be better brought this project to life. And to Yelena Nesbit, Rebecca Raskin, and the entire team at Harper Wave who continue to offer your expertise, thank you.

Endless, hugest gratitude and love to my husband, Mitch, who's cooked meals, listened, and critiqued tirelessly during the writing of this book. And to our three boys Reid, Max, and Zac, thank you for the blessing of your presence in my life, my inspiring, courageous, insightful boys. Love you so very much.

Elena would like to thank her dad, mom, sister, and family, as well as Dr. Anthony Lyon, James Benard, Jonah Lyon, Dr. Gabrielle Lyon, Yogarupa Rod Stryker, Dr. Douglas Brooks, Lauren Zander, Marnie Nir, Beth Weissenberger, Dana Bauer, Anna Walko, and Niki Morrisette for their unwavering presence and care.

Resources

———

Elena and I have compiled a concise but thorough list of resources to help you navigate the coming months and years, for yourself and for your family. Our intent is to leave you feeling full of supportive, constructive ideas with which you can go forward. Each of these authors has provided us with foundational insights. We've used these books to enrich our practices, our writings, and our work with our clients.

Gabrielle Bernstein, *May Cause Miracles: A 40-Day Guidebook of Subtle Shifts for Radical Change and Unlimited Happiness* (New York: Harmony Books, 2013) and *Judgment Detox: Release the Beliefs That Hold You Back from Living A Better Life* (New York: Gallery Books, 2018)

Where you place your attention, you amplify. With accessible language and practices, Bernstein ushers you into a place of forgiving your thoughts, clearing out even the most insidious, habitual judgments, and releasing beliefs that hold you back from your highest possibilities. Acceptance, nonjudgment, creativity, choice, and the freedom that ensues are all elements of her work, which includes EFT, meditation, practical prayers, and journaling. Bernstein invites you to quantifiably shift your energy in order to shift your (and your family's) future.

Brené Brown, ***Rising Strong: The Reckoning, the Rumble, the Revolution*** (New York: Spiegel & Grau, 2015) and ***Braving the Wilderness: The Quest for True Belonging and the Courage to Stand Alone*** (New York: Random House, 2017)

When I became curious about vulnerability, a dear friend suggested I take a look at Brené Brown's work. Vulnerability is what makes us human; is helpful to consider in the context of divorce resolution. *Rising Strong* takes the examination a step further, as Brown examines courage, vulnerability, shame, and worthiness. Vulnerability is the willingness to show up and be seen with no guarantee of outcome—and it's the only path to more love, belonging, creativity, and joy. *Rising Strong* is a study of the rise from the fall.

In *Braving the Wilderness*, Brown offers a definition of true belonging that might surprise you, and it will likely help you feel far more connected and purposeful in moments of doubt and loneliness than ever before. Her compelling childhood stories will help you feel included, seen, and felt. This book is an invitation to explore how you belong to yourself. Her potent reminder is that your willingness to choose courage over comfort will determine the course of your life.

Bill Burnett and Dave Evans, ***Designing Your Life: How to Build a Well-Built Joyful Life*** (New York: Knopf, 2016)

We can create a life that is meaningful and fulfilling no matter who we are. Our age, accomplishments, and station in life do not limit where we can go. Approaching life as one would a design challenge, each one of us has the opportunity to build a satisfying, meaningful life. The message delivered is that the only failure is settling for a life that does not make us happy. This book provides a clear, iterative process for navigating yourself forward.

Pema Chödrön, ***When Things Fall Apart: Heart Advice for Difficult Times*** (Boulder, CO: Shambhala, 2016; anniversary ed.) and ***The Wisdom of No Escape and the Path of Loving-Kindness*** (Boulder, CO: Shambhala, 2001)

Through traditional Buddhist wisdom, Pema Chödrön examines the issue of truly living your life even when it seems to be crumbling. How do we move forward when we feel overcome with fear, anxiety, and pain? Pema suggests that moving toward our difficult situation and becoming intimate with our pain allows heartful opening. She offers life-changing tools for transforming suffering and negative patterns into habitual ease and boundless joy. In *Wisdom*, she explores the Four Noble Truths of Buddhism and the practice of *tonglen* in real terms, imploring you to use your daily life to stay curious, spacious, and awake to the interconnectedness of all things, in both your interactions and your state of mind.

Amy Cuddy, ***Presence: Bringing Your Boldest Self to Your Biggest Challenges*** (New York: Back Bay Books, 2015) and **"Power Poses"** (TED Talk, 2012)

I was first introduced to Amy Cuddy at a dinner party when a friend suggested that her TED Talk, "Your Body Language May Shape Who You Are," would be great for my nervous clients just before entering a meeting, a negotiation, or the courtroom. The talk is about power poses, and the theory is that by accessing our personal power, we can achieve presence. A sense of presence adjusts the impression we make on ourselves, and then translates forward into the world, informing how we are perceived. While the science underlying Dr. Cuddy's theories has recently been called into question, by altering our body language, we can shift our mindset, our behavior, and the outcome.

Susan David, ***Emotional Agility: Get Unstuck, Embrace Change, and Thrive in Work and Life*** (New York: Avery, 2016)
This is a practical, science-based guide to looking within and living with intent. Recognize your emotions, accept them, learn from them, and become more resilient no matter where you are in your process.

Carol Dweck, ***Mindset: The New Psychology of Success*** (New York: Ballantine Books, 2007)
According to Dweck's research, individuals can be placed on a continuum according to their implicit assumptions about ability. Some believe their success is based on innate, built-in ability; these folks are said to have a "fixed" mindset. Those who believe their success is based on hard work, learning, training, and doggedness are said to have a "growth" mindset. Whether we realize it or not, our mindset is especially evident in our reaction to failure. Fixed-mindset individuals dread failure because they perceive failure to be a negative reflection of their basic abilities, while growth-mindset individuals realize that failure is a process of learning how to improve and refine their performance. The mindset you exhibit plays a vital role in all aspects of your life. Dweck posits that cultivating a growth mindset will allow you to live a less stressful and more successful life.

Howard Glasser and Jennifer Easley, ***Transforming the Difficult Child: The Nurtured Heart Approach*** (Tucson, AZ: Nurtured Heart Publications, 1998)
Designed to build character strengths and virtues using positive psychology, the Nurtured Heart Approach is a social-emotional strategy used to transform negative behaviors into positive behaviors and to increase connectivity among family members. Some-

times even the calmest of children can act out during difficult times; the wisdom in this book will help you manage those moments. With an emphasis on noticing the neutral as a tool to shift negative behaviors and reactions, this approach is useful for shifting the dynamic with a difficult ex as well.

Thich Nhat Hanh, *Anger: Wisdom for Cooling the Flames* (New York: Riverhead Books, 2002)
Thich Nhat Hanh teaches you to relax the bonds of attachment, anger, and delusion through mindfulness and kindness toward yourself. According to this beloved teacher of meditation, "Many people look for happiness outside themselves, but true happiness must come from inside of us. Our culture tells us that happiness comes from having a lot of money, a lot of power, and a high position in society. But if you observe carefully, you will see that many rich and famous people are not happy." Thich Nhat Hanh's teachings usher us from the internal swirl and external whirl toward deep calm. According to the Dalai Lama, Thich Nhat Hanh shows us the connection between personal inner peace and peace on earth.

Marie Kondo, *The Life-Changing Magic of Tidying Up: The Japanese Art of Decluttering and Organizing* (New York: Ten Speed Press, 2014)
Tossing and donating piles of belongings for both Elena and me has created space that effectively cleared our minds and our homes. This book is a game changer. Marie Kondo gives step-by-step guidance for determining the items in your environment that "spark joy" and ridding yourself of all that does not. According to Kondo, when we release belongings that no longer serve us, we make space for what brings us clarity. When you clear your clutter, she shows, you'll enjoy a calm, motivated mindset. Making space in your physical

environment is another means by which you can shift your life in a more positive direction.

Harold S. Kushner, ***Nine Essential Things I've Learned About Life*** (New York: Knopf, 2015)
Rabbi Harold Kushner condenses his experiences as a rabbi into nine essential points. Especially relevant at any point during your divorce process are the stories about personal strength in forgiveness. This is a fresh, vital offering of belief, mercy, conscience, and strength delivered with pragmatic advice, including reflections to consider. Rooted in Kushner's capacity to weave history and scripture with popular culture, this book is an illuminating, useful, quick read.

William Martin, ***The Parent's Tao Te Ching*** (Cambridge, MA: Da Capo Press, 1999)
Martin distills the essence of the Tao's eighty-one chapters as they relate to parenting. Without being overly instructive, this book is a potent collection of teachings: how to respond without judgment, how to emulate natural processes, and how to balance doing with being.

Wendy Mogel, PhD, ***The Blessing of a Skinned Knee*** (New York: Scribner, 2001) and ***Voice Lessons for Parents*** (New York: Scribner, 2018)
Drawing on the wisdom of the Torah, the Talmud, and other teachings, *The Blessing of a Skinned Knee* uses the framework of nine blessings to help parents prioritize and cultivate positivity, help kids accept themselves, and help all learn to appreciate our many blessings. In *Voice Lessons*, Mogel elaborates on each stage and age of a

child's development, bringing to light the chances you have to connect through language, to sort through the most uncomfortable topics and create a lasting connection with your kids through this time.

Rabbi Perry Netter, *Divorce Is a Mitzvah: A Practical Guide to Finding Wholeness and Holiness When Your Marriage Dies* (Woodstock, VT: Jewish Lights Publishing, 2002)
Divorced father, pastoral counselor, and congregational rabbi Netter illustrates how wholeness and holiness can be found in divorce and separation. He offers practical wisdom, information, and strength from a Jewish perspective to guide you through this challenging life transition. He explores the transformation of moving through trauma into a lifetime of growth and greater spiritual understanding.

Kate Northrup, *Money, A Love Story* (Carlsbad, CA: Hay House, 2013)
Northrup untangles your financial woes and helps you be a conduit for the life you want. As money is really an arbitrary system, your work is to begin re-creating your relationship to it from the ground up, through journaling, patching leaks, and vigilant explorations of how you spend and save. Northrup is here to help you take inventory of your blessings and learn how to pay your future self by the choices you make today. Let her help you redefine wealth and become friends with your abundant self. Especially if money is scary for you, this is a must on your list.

Mark Nepo, *Things That Join the Sea and the Sky* (Boulder, CO: Sounds True, 2017)
Elena loves Nepo's short prose reflections on life, love, and listening. This is a rich resource of reading and inquiry, to help recalibrate

any difficult moment with the help of Nepo's post-cancer perspective, and reconfigure your relations with yourself and those closest to you.

Esther Perel, **Mating in Captivity** (New York: Harper Paperbacks, 2017) and **The State of Affairs** (New York: Harper, 2017)
Esther Perel has officially opened the conversation around the feasibility of modern human monogamy. What does it mean to balance the need for intimacy, love, belonging, and security with the need for freedom, adventure, and the exploration of erotic desire? Her writing and her talks are real, refreshing, and raw as she unearths the unspoken truths around marriage, love, and fidelity. According to Perel, an affair is not to be judged, and it needn't end your marriage. In fact, for some it can actually create a new beginning, as it refines each party's role and redefines the marriage relationship. Her TED Talks are powerful and full of interesting perspective. Be sure to check out "The Secret to Desire in a Long-Term Relationship" and "Rethinking Infidelity—A Talk for Anyone Who Has Ever Loved."

Jillian Pransky, **Deep Listening** (New York: Rodale Books, 2017)
Accessible, profound, and clear, the wisdom of *Deep Listening* grants us a chance to greet our habitual stress with new eyes of kindness and compassion. Through concise, consistent, and cumulative practices, Jillian provides us with the context to live more openheartedly and transform our ways of seeing and being. Pransky doesn't ask you to "be your best self" or "do more!" She asks you to "be here" and "do less," from being present and noticing your tension to welcoming what you discover with compassion. She integrates guided meditations, journaling prompts, and re-

storative yoga poses to help you regard yourself with kindness and curiosity.

Gretchen Rubin, ***The Happiness Project: Or, Why I Spent a Year Trying to Sing in the Morning, Clean My Closets, Fight Right, Read Aristotle, and Generally Have More Fun*** (New York: Harper Paperbacks, 2015) and ***Better Than Before: What I Learned About Making and Breaking Habits—To Sleep More, Quit Sugar, Procrastinate Less, and Generally Build a Happier Life*** (New York: Crown, 2015)

The Happiness Project by Gretchen Rubin provides an uplifting post-divorce read. Gretchen Rubin says, "Time is passing, and I'm not focusing enough on the things that really matter." With that, she dedicated a year to studying happiness. She explores various tracks, testing out current happiness research, age-old wisdom, and pop culture happiness tips. She brings humor and insight into this uplifting, interesting, and helpful book, which is full of surprising tips. The smallest changes can make the biggest differences. In *Better Than Before*, Gretchen explores the idea of making things automatic by creating conscious habits. These books are useful for a deeper understanding of the myriad unconscious choices we make, and how to shift them.

Dr. Stuart Shanker, ***Self-Reg: How to Help Your Child (and You) Break the Stress Cycle and Successfully Engage with Life*** (New York: Penguin, 2017)

It's challenging for parents to truly grasp the various unseen stressors with which kids, and especially teens, are struggling. In this groundbreaking book, you'll learn how to regulate yourself, recover, and respond to your own hidden stressors so you can help mitigate the experience your kids are having. This book is a welcome tool for any parent.

Jen Sincero, *You Are a Badass: How to Stop Doubting Your Greatness and Start Living an Awesome Life* (New York: Running Press, 2013)

This book is a perfect companion to *Better Apart*. Jen Sincero delivers a solid plan for how to get from where you are to where you want to go. Feisty, saucy, and humorous, Sincero explores personal power, gratitude, forgiveness, meditation, the banishing of fear, and learning from experiences. She is totally relatable and does a great job making the reader feel empowered to take on the world and make life happen. The primary message is that the universe will give us all we desire as long as we are focused and committed to doing the work to make the magic happen.

Susan Squire, *I Don't: A Contrarian History of Marriage* (New York: Bloomsbury USA, 2008)

For those of us inclined to study human relationships, Susan Squire's provocative survey of marriage and what it has meant for society, politics, religion, and the home elucidates the turbulent history of the basic institution of marriage, now ten thousand years old. Starting with the discovery, long before recorded time, that sex leads to paternity (and hence to couplehood), and leading up to the dawn of the modern "love marriage," Squire delves into the many ways men and women have come together, and what the state of their unions has meant for history, society, and politics—especially the politics of the home. This book is rooted in more than a decade's research, but even more compelling is the author's contrarian boldness. *I Don't* is a compelling read for all thinkers: feminists, traditionalists, conservatives, and progressives alike.

Dr. Brian Weiss, ***Many Lives, Many Masters: The True Story of a Prominent Psychiatrist, His Young Patient, and the Past-Life Therapy That Changed Both Their Lives*** (New York: Fireside, 1988)
In Brian Weiss's bestseller *Many Lives, Many Masters*, he introduces the reader to his patient, Catherine. In a hypnotic state, Dr. Weiss's young patient summoned memories of many past lifetimes, demonstrated an astonishing ability to transmit transcendental messages, and turned the life of a respectable psychiatrist upside down. Weiss studied at Columbia University and at the Yale School of Medicine (1970), where he later completed his psychiatry residency. For many years he served as the head of psychiatry at Mount Sinai Medical Center. Weiss advocates hypnotic regression as therapy, claiming that many phobias and ailments are rooted in past-life experiences, which can have a curative effect. He offers workshops and seminars across the United States that explain and teach self-regression meditation techniques. During times of great stress, you may find Dr. Weiss's work incredibly healing and supportive. Worth a read if you are open to alternative explanations of how and why things happen as they do within a spiritual construct.

Lauren Zander, ***Maybe It's You: Cut the Crap. Face Your Fears. Love Your Life.*** (New York: Hachette, 2017)
Maybe It's You picks up where *You Are a Badass* leaves off. It's a no-nonsense, practical manual to help you figure out what you want out of life and how to actually get there. Zander walks you through her efficacious, innovative process, revealing results that can be achieved when you stop lying to yourself and begin keeping your promises. Through practical exercises, client stories, and Lauren's own hard-won lessons, this book will enable you to identify, articulate, and account for your own personal setbacks so you can transform them into strengths.

Elizabeth Thayer, PhD, and Jeffrey Zimmerman, PhD, **The Co-Parenting Survival Guide: Letting Go of Conflict After a Difficult Divorce** (Oakland, CA: New Harbinger Publications, 2001)
In the county in which I practice divorce law, this guidebook is strongly suggested reading for the compulsory parenting course provided to all separating parents. *The Co-Parenting Survival Guide* illustrates how to navigate post-separation parenting within two households, identifying and resolving common hostility traps, with useful tools for sustaining a co-parenting partnership based on love and concern for your children.

About the Authors

———

GABRIELLE HARTLEY is an attorney, mediator, consultant, speaker, and author. She served as court attorney for Judge Jeffrey Sunshine in New York City matrimonial court and is a member of the Massachusetts Council on Family Mediation, the Hampshire County Bar Association, and the family law section of the New York State Bar Association. She lives in Northampton, Massachusetts, with her husband and three sons. Mediate or consult with Gabrielle via yourelegantdivorce.com.

ELENA BROWER is a teacher, author, and speaker who has taught yoga and meditation since 1999. She is the bestselling author of *Practice You: A Journal*, and her first book, *Art of Attention*, has been translated into six languages. Elena has contributed to *Yoga Journal*, *Yoga International*, the *Huffington Post*, *MindBodyGreen*, Well + Good NYC, Positively Positive, and other outlets. Practice with Elena on YogaGlo.com.